truly tiny
gardens

Caroline Gunter

Photographer Leigh Clapp

Acknowledgements

The author, photographer and publisher wish to thank the following garden designers, nurseries and garden owners for their permission to feature the gardens in this book.

Garden Designers

Ann-Marie & Dror Barkai, Qld (pages 4, 51, 96 left); Botanix, Vic (page 26); Colin Branch, NSW (page 54, bottom); Greg Boyer, Hawaii (pages 64, 66); Michael Cooke, NSW (pages 43 bottom, 68 top, 92 bottom, 102 top right); Rick Eckersley, Vic (front cover, page 98 bottom right); Faulkner & Chapman, Vic (pages 28, 81); Marcia Hosking, NSW (page 90 bottom right); Peter Fudge, NSW (pages 33, 52 top, 56, 75 top, 95 right); Imperial Gardens, NSW (pages 7, 101 bottom right); Sue Isherwood, NSW (pages 59 bottom, 61 top & bottom, 72 top); Katisma Landscaping, NSW (pages 12, 72 bottom, 73, 102 bottom right); Marc Peter Keane, Kyoto (pages 40, 41); Darryl Mappin, Qld (pages 30, 31, 74); Rupert McGregor Landscapes, Tas (page 52 bottom); Ronni Nettleton, Vic (page 88, bottom right); Ann-Maree O'Brien, Landscaper, Tas (pages 50 top, 82 top); Patio, NSW (pages 27, 92 left); Christine Pearson, NSW (pages 25, 57); Andrew Prowse, Qld (page 94, top right); Penny Ruddock, SA (page 69); Secret Gardens of Sydney, NSW (pages 22, 23, 85 top, 91 bottom, 94 top left, 101 top); Carol Shuler, Arizona (page 50 bottom); Matthew Taylor, NSW (page 8); Margaret Wright, SA (page 10).

Gardens/Garden Owners

Albion Farm, NSW (page 105 middle); Jude Alcorn (pages 14, 15); Bernard Bolan, NSW (page 55); Phillip Bull, NSW (pages 85, 104); Barbara Clare, NSW (pages 90 top right, 91 top); Corinda, Tas (pages 58, 88 top right); Deauville gardens, NSW (pages 36, 37, 48, 49, 62); Dunedin, Tas (page 79); Hillcrest, NSW (page 67 right); Doug Hirst, Qld (page 42); Kaye Leighton, NSW (page 44 top); Morgan garden, Tas (pages 38, 90 middle); Jann News, NSW (page 46); Pondokkie, NSW (pages 17 top, 24 bottom, 98 top, 105 bottom left); Pukekura Park, NSW (page 83); Red Cow Farm, NSW (pages 59 top, 70, 76); Rose Briar Cottage, NSW (page 17 bottom); The Secret Garden, NSW (page 88, left); Secull garden, Vic (page 98 bottom left); Seddon garden, WA (pages 68 bottom, 75 bottom).

Nurseries/Businesses

David Mackay Harrison, Sculptor, NSW (page 92 bottom); Lambley Nursery, Vic (page 94 bottom left); Bali in Profile, NSW (pages 34, 35, 105 top right); Plant Hunter's Nursery, Tas (page 90 bottom left).

The author particularly wishes to thank Rob Willis of Belrose Nursery, NSW, for all his help.

contents

planning
a truly tiny
garden

This book is for those who've just
acquired a truly tiny garden, or who
have been ruefully viewing an exisiting
one – or even an undeveloped corner –
that needs a revamp or perhaps a
whole new impetus.

At left is a tiny tropical waterway. Inside
are many alternative exquisite scenes
to suit a variety of different sites,
geographic situations and climates.
Read on and be inspired.

the advantages
of small spaces

Yes, it is small. But it holds both gigantic benefits and heaps of potential.

First in the way of benefits, because it's small it's easy to maintain. In a tiny garden, a quick circuit armed with a digger, a cutter and a light bucket or an old plastic pot for the spoils, and it's returned to perfection. It bounces back to just the way it was planned to look. In slightly larger but still small gardens, regular tidying won't take much longer. Take note, I did say regular. Leave it too long and it will become a bit more of a task. But there won't be difficult corners to negotiate, wheelbarrows to trundle and assorted tools to use, lose and then have to find again.

Secondly, disposing of the collection of trimmings is an easily managed task. Cut them small and they easily fit in a small compost bin or worm farm to become material that will benefit your garden. Or store the waste in a tidy vegetation-recycling bin available from most progressive city councils.

Thirdly, tasks are not so daunting in a small area. To sweep the paving, paint the fence or the lattice and to replant the garden beds can be arranged and completed in no time. There won't be half-finished jobs waiting for tomorrow, next weekend or the first fine day.

Fourth benefit: planning and shopping for a small area means, simply, less money has to be spent. You just don't need to buy as much as those with large gardens. You can create a terrific effect on a limited budget. If funds allow it, extravagant decisions in the way of quality paving, the choice of an advanced tree or series of shrubs for a hedge, the purchase of rare or unusual plants, or the selection of a fabulous feature become real possibilities.

For benefit number five, you can carry home with you the bags of fertiliser and additives needed to keep the soil in top-notch condition. Storing them and your garden tools requires merely a corner in a cupboard or an empty garden pot.

And for number six, when you have to water the garden, you will of course use much less water, an essential consideration in modern resources management. Fitting a watering system is a snap, requiring just so much less in the way of piping and fixtures. Often, a water feature playing in a confined area will splash or simply increase the humidity sufficiently to keep moisture loving plants quite content.

But all these benefits do not come without counter-balances. To make a tiny garden a success requires careful assessment and planning before its true potential can be realised.

garden assessment

OPPOSITE A strong pink Easter/Michaelmas daisy *Aster novae-angliae* cultivar on the left is teamed with *Aster* 'Silver Spray' separated by a toning echinacea. These perennials put on a generous late summer/early autumn show but look attractive all year.

ABOVE A water feature such as this is an easy care addition to any tiny space. Here a small courtyard space has been planted with the black bamboo, *Phyllostachys nigra*, and the reedy grass, *Acorus calamus*. Both are beautifully manageable and will need little upkeep except for an occasional pruning back of bamboo canes. An alternative planting which would add an interesting gold variegation to the scene would be to use the variegated species of both plants – *Bambusa multiplex* 'Golden Goddess' and *Acorus calamus* 'Variegatus'.

Look at the size and shape of your small garden. It may well be a tiny city rectangle or a long narrow slice, bordered on three sides by fences. It may be a courtyard, deck or rooftop space that is often the only outside patch of fresh air allotted to multiple dwellings. It could be the space at the back of the house that, although small, is where the washing dries, barbecues are cooked, children play, bikes and cars are stored and the bins, recycling materials and "junk" sit waiting. Crammed and glowering.

All these sites have the potential to become an intimate enclosure, a refuge, a cosy spot out of the wind or a shaded retreat from the baking sun – and all, a pleasure to view and use.

Next assess the surroundings. There may be towering slabs of walls either dauntingly blank or relieved by windows and decks that all share an overhead view of your garden.

There may be a mishmash of fencing styles, heights and additions that can create problems to be solved along your edge-lines.

There will often be an unsightly immovable object like a towering tree, an outdoor shed or a large building in your space, or nearby, that may swamp your site with shade, block an outlook or loom dominantly over you. Most councils have tree preservation orders to aid greenhouse gas reduction and maintenance of wildlife habitat, and, unless the tree is classified as a noxious weed or its roots are posing problems or danger to the area, you may well have to live with it. A qualified arboriculturist can provide thinning and shaping services, reducing the bulk of the tree while maintaining its integrity. Simple tree-lopping is not the answer and will only disfigure the tree's form, leaving you with a dispirited eyesore and diminishing the benefits its preservation would provide. All cities need trees.

An immovable structural eyesore can only be disguised or turned into a feature.

And while on the subject of shade, the next observation has to be about the sun, or lack of it, that reaches your tiny kingdom. It should take the whole year to assess conditions, but new owners are not often willing to wait that long. Local weather bureaus, council consultants, garden designers and the locals will most likely be able to fill you in. Often, because of the smallness of the site and height of surrounding structures, the sun may travel only a tiny path across your patch. The summer sun may reach in but the low winter angle may preclude it. Don't try to grow sun-loving plants in these conditions – they'll just become pale, weak and leggy and look pathetic. On the other hand, if your site is a sun-blazened desert zone throughout the day, plant the sun-worshippers, remember to water them regularly and erect some screens for shade protection so you can enjoy it too. A pergola or trellis covered with deciduous vines will provide winter sun and summer shade.

ABOVE A shapely Japanese maple is centred in a chequerboard design with squares of mondo grass in shade and lamb's ears on the sunny side. Scarlet passion flower, *Passiflora coccinea*, weaves up the lattice walls creating a linked fence treatment.
This modern "parterre" is easy to achieve and maintain and could be a tidy solution for a small courtyard or entry garden.

OPPOSITE Colour and form bear close inspection in small spaces. Making the most of a dry sunny mound, the flowering plumes of *Pennisetum alopecuroides* and a rigid bearded iris provide contrasting forms and toning colours, while a splash of yellow kalanchoe between complements them brilliantly. The spears of the grass and the blades of the the iris are strong shapes providing interest in a corner even when they are not in flower.

Lattice, bamboo blinds, batten slats and retractable awnings are other alternatives. They will also screen you from observation from buildings above.

Observe the wind patterns that batter your block. Narrow spaces between the solidity of buildings become wind tunnels in a strong wind and create a draught in mild conditions. Decks on tall blocks of housing will catch every breeze that blows, while edges of valleys and exposed positions in the teeth of prevailing winds get more than a fair share of wind buffeting.

The native or surviving vegetation demonstrates nature's coping strategies and to help your garden survive you'd do well to copy them. Grow leafy screens that will break up the draught and direct it over the top. Plant strong-leafed, wind-tolerant varieties, such as oleander, olive, broom, bamboo, coast banksia, shore pines or New Zealand Christmas tree in the front line to filter the wind, leafy shrubs as a second barrier, and those that requiring delicate swaddling in their lee.

Semi-permeable fencing, battens or lattice are man-made devices that will produce a similar effect. These can be thickened and greened with twining vines or espaliered shrubs.

planning

What do you want from your garden?

Should it screen your house and windows from passers-by? Do you want to feel that once you're home you can close the door and be cocooned, private and comfy in your snug world?

Or do you hanker for outdoor living space in a private courtyard where there's a spot for reading the paper in the morning sun, a seat for morning or afternoon tea, a table for a candlelit dinner or room to stretch out in the sun?

Perhaps you'd just like space for a private showcase of a well-tended gardening arrangement, a water feature for its soothing effect, or a scene to be viewed from inside the house?

All these sorts of gardens protect the house from the busyness of the world outside and help to create a private retreat.

And then there are gardens designed to be viewed from the street. Both flowers and foliage create a spectacular display that is generously shared.

These gardens can be an essential part in decorating and dressing the house, perhaps picking up the colours of the paintwork, framing the windows, leading the way to the door. They can even be used to disguise shortcomings.

Perhaps your garden needs to be a family area, with space organised to fit multiple needs.

Make a list of your preferences and sort them in order of priority. Use inspiration and advice from friends and decide realistically what is practical for your lifestyle, your site and its surroundings. Think laterally about requirements that your local park might fulfil and remember that your needs will change. Your tiny garden can develop and change to keep step and because it's small, it's not an enormous task to redirect or redesign it.

what's best
in a small
garden

Keep it simple. Complicated arrangements in a small space are unsettling. The eye cannot move smoothly over a scene where there are too many distractions.

Select a style, a mood, an impression and keep to it. Don't "muddy" the effect of, say, a classic formal design, by adding something like a Balinese corner after a holiday there. Gardeners with large spaces can arrange a series of garden rooms but your small plot is better as one single space which both displays your taste and meets your needs.

Keep things in scale with the size of the garden.

In a small area, over-scaled trees, walls and features look inappropriate and overwhelming, tending to accentuate the smallness of the site. A large tree will fill the garden with its shade, fallen leaves, trunk and its roots. See pages 118-119 for a list of suitable trees.

A grand statue or water feature will dominate and leave insufficient space around for either viewing it or setting it off. On the other hand, lots of tiny pieces tend to look bitty and muddled. One medium sized feature will become the focal point and will have more impact as it draws the eye to it.

The impression of space expands a tiny site. Keep plantings back against the walls or, if central, keep them low so there will always be an openness about the design. Plants will naturally lean from a wall and will need regular trimming or they'll not only restrict access but overwhelm the whole garden. They'll make it seem smaller than it actually is. If you've got a significant tree, carefully cut off its low branches so space is perceivable under the leaf canopy.

Tricks and illusions can help to make a small area seem much larger than it really is.

Pale, cool flowers like blue, mauve and lime-white recede, whereas bright colours, like red, orange and yellow, leap forward. However, if you love to use the brights, combine them in a massed planting where they become a single entity rather than individual exclamation marks.

Use light green, grey or pale-lime foliage instead of deep green, bright yellow or vibrant red, which will just leap out at you. Shiny foliage however, will reflect the light and reduce the size and dominance of the plant.

Fine-textured foliage seems to move away from the viewer, whereas large-leafed forms appear to move forward. They can be used to make a garden look bigger if there are large leaves, say at the gate and small-leafed specimens at the far end. However, conceal large-leafed plants behind a small-leafed one if you want to use the effect in reverse. Large-leafed plants work well as space dividers, beckoning you around a corner to the "enormous" space beyond where small-leafed specimens abound. A complete hedge of fine-textured plants recedes miraculously, but the effect will be simply boring if used exclusively.

Where the space is long and narrow you'll only increase the effect if you run paths, gardens or columns of shrubs lengthwise down the site. Even paving patterns running lengthways extend the impression. To reduce it, lay gardens and paving across the site where possible.

Aim for light-coloured and simple paving. The colours of light marble, concrete blocks and sand-coloured pavers will expand the area whereas dark pavers, such as slate or deep red terracotta will contract it. Patterned paving also appears to reduce the space.

Mirrors in the garden can deceive the eye and increase the light in a small area. When set directly on a wall they reflect and expand the garden. When surrounded by an archway or pergola and wrapped in greenery, they give the impression of more garden beyond. Make sure you hang them sloping in from the top or leave them easily movable so the sun will not shine directly onto them and uncomfortably into your eyes as it changes position with the seasons. Use heavy-duty glass for safety and waterproof the edges to protect the backing.

RIGHT Elegant *Magnolia stellata* blooms dress bare stems just when needed in late winter/early spring and have the added attraction of being sweetly perfumed. Where space is limited, plants that provide multiple pleasures are a bonus.

OPPOSITE Here contrasts of foliage and form create a simple and strong garden design. Included are balls of box, a sea of grey santolina, a central and end hedge of *Hebe buxifolia*, soft curves of purple-flowering raphiolepis and exclamation points of conifers.

solving the problem

On the following pages we've pictured and described various small gardens that have solved problems for their owners and turned tiny areas into a pleasure, both to use and to view. We anticipate they will set you thinking, imagining and planning what your tiny garden can become. You can copy these plantings to the letter, but because nature follows its own path, each garden will develop differently. You might like to mix and match sections to suit your scene or simply use the ideas pictured to create your own arrangement of plants or features.

If your budget will allow it, employ a qualified designer who will listen to your requirements, assess the problems and help you achieve your dreams. Their expertise isn't cheap but they can save you a great deal of trial and error and expensive failures.

And don't forget, small can be just great.

the outdoor room

By dressing an outdoor area with all the charm, style and practicality that you've displayed inside, you create another room, a real extension of your living area. A shading umbrella, a vine-clad pergola or rain-proof protection will make it useable for much of the year.

It can become an alternative outdoor lounge and/or dining room, a sheltered retreat from the noise and bustle of a busy life, a functional space for household tasks, a play area for children or an artistic arrangement of plants with an ornament or a water feature.

A happy combination of all is pictured left.

LEFT Waterproofing, an essential of rooftop gardening, is provided by an impermeable film beneath the paving. Generously-sized pots provide attractive and stable sites for citrus and herbs – year-round marjoram, thyme and rosemary – with fragrant summer basil added seasonally. A passionfruit vine, productively nourished in a large pot, meanders along the parapet. A well-secured pot holds petunias adding a splash of colour to this end of the garden.

OPPOSITE ABOVE Durable furniture increases the value of an outdoor room. A market umbrella will provide sun-shelter. It's wise to use heavy furniture and weighted umbrella bases on exposed sites as wind gusts can play havoc with anything flimsy.

OPPOSITE BELOW Wind-break, privacy screening and perfume are all provided by murrayas with lavenders, a rose and a brunfelsia in front. Parsley, varietal lettuces, chives, society garlic and tomatoes romp in a built-up bed, together with colourful snapdragons, salvias, poppies, petunias and shrubby regal pelargoniums.

GROUND RULES

Make sure the soil is a lightweight mix if there are structures below and feed it generously four times a year to support such productive growth as shown here.

room
at the top

When you live high in the sky you can easily observe the weather but are usually well clear of the growing side of nature. It's rare to see greenery on your level. There are the difficulties of transporting pots, soil mixes, plants and equipment to the site, of guaranteeing safe and adequate drainage and protection for the properties below and coping with the wind and blazing sun. But this gardener has created a visual feast – and a culinary one as well, with herbs, fruit and vegetables parading with scented flowers to define this deliciously inviting room.

cool verandahs

The shady protection of a verandah offers many possibilities. Roofed and partially windowed, it can become a year-round room. As an entrance, it can be dressed to become decorative and welcoming. When it's level with the floor inside, it expands and opens up the adjacent rooms. And its protection will allow you to grow plants that aren't possible outdoors. Conceal in boxes or seats the meters and water heaters that are often housed on a verandah, and provide baskets or hooks for the paraphernalia usually discarded at the door, and you'll have made a start to turning it into a room.

ABOVE Lush tropical treasures that will survive even cool areas through summer in the protection of a verandah include aglaonema, bird's-nest fern, philadendrons, white-flowered madonna lily and a red-flowered spathiphyllum. Eucharist lily and maidenhair fern rest on pebbles in saucers of water to maintain humidity.

OPPOSITE A deck level with the floor inside and generously wide door openings allow the verandah and room to become one. The pergola draped in potato vine and twined in variegated ivy enhances and maintains a cooling effect.

RIGHT In winter, enclosed verandahs provide a snug retreat, ideal for the display of flowering orchids moved in from outside. Begonias and ferns are the year-round dwellers with the begonia flowering in a softly nodding display for about two months.

GROUND RULES
Plants that will flower in some shade, like begonias and impatiens, will need morning or afternoon sun to keep them blooming.

GROUND RULES
The creeping fig, while a reliably fast-growing plant to cover walls in shade, demands regular clipping every month to prevent it escaping to large leaf growth. A less demanding alternative would be a small-leafed ivy. Standard roses, like the Iceberg shown here, are most vigorous when pruned back annually to 5cm above the graft.

LEFT Creeping fig and boughs of climbing roses screen the lattice wall extension. The trickling fountain gurgles gently and provides water for birds. Above it nestles a pull-out clothesline that is fixed, when needed, to the opposite wall. Gardenias, violets, lavender and a leggy 'Iceberg' rose provide perfume.

OPPOSITE The terracotta pool edge gives enough room for access, maintenance, and the softening clutch of pots – a lime, orchids and a clipped fig. The wall at left is draped in climbing roses with summer-flowering agapanthus at their feet. Remember when planting near a pool that filter baskets will need constant clearing of petals and falling leaves. Note the generously opening double doors that let the outside in.

dining
or diving

This tiny inner-city garden, 10m x 6m, has a place for everything. There's a small pool, fenced for safety and raised on a terrace to minimise excavation intrusion. This also allows maximum sun to warm the water. Raised beds and pots provide flowers for the house, perfume for the garden and herbs for the kitchen. Paving presents an area to dry the washing, space for the dogs to sunbake and for the family to read and dine. Privacy is assured with high fencing fronted by an ample hedging of murrayas, sasanqua camellias and a climbing rose.

GROUND RULES
If space is too limited
for dedicated play areas,
remember the hose can also
be a great source of summer
pleasure and simply helping
to water the pots can be
instructive fun.

LEFT A corner of the yard, edged
off and deeply mulched with fine
bark or leaf, makes for clean play
and safe landings. Be sure to
position stepping stones well
away from swings and climbing
equipment and keep the cover
thick around footings. A cubby
house is useful for rainy days
and secret games and can be
converted to a pirate or space
ship or a sleep-over site as
children become more adventurous.
An outside table at child height
is useful for messy stuff, such as
water play and painting, as well
as tea parties.

OPPOSITE The simplest equipment
can be all you need. A frame,
generously filled with sand and
some containers, spoons or
purpose-made gear, will provide
hours of entertainment and
learning for small children. Spend
some time out there with them so
it becomes a shared enjoyment.
Always cover the sand with a
waterproof screen after the kids
have left so it remains clean and
dry and animals can't soil it.

places for play

A spot where young children can be watched at play and that is hazard-free is an important addition to a small family garden. Parks are for wilder running, biking and tree climbing, and will usually have a collection of play equipment. At home, a box of sand, a swing or a cubby house will provide hours of imaginative and creative play when trips out aren't possible. Position the play area under deciduous shelter if your winters are cool and where, for summer, there'll be shade. Check regularly that the equipment is safe and that there aren't spider and mosquito colonies, both of which make things less than pleasant.

greek
inspiration

Here a tiny back garden has been walled for privacy then painted and decorated to create the look of a Greek taverna – and the lowest of low maintenance gardens. Sparkling white walls and "stone" floor combine to enlarge the area and the vivid blue shutters, door and furnishings echo the tile trim at the barbecue. Great pots of bright geraniums and herbs all shout of the Mediterranean. An olive tree in a corner and a grape vine set to clamber around the pergola will complete the scene in a couple of years. You can almost hear the music and dancing ...

BELOW LEFT This olive tree will grow to shade the barbecue chef at work and will, over time, assume an attractive shape but not an overpowering size.

OPPOSITE ABOVE LEFT Sage, chives, parsley and basil tumble from a planter box at the kitchen window, with society garlic at their feet. Bright colours are added with sweet William and a wall basket filled with rich red ivy geranium that will cascade over the pot.

OPPOSITE ABOVE RIGHT In a boundary wall, "window" niches with shutters break up the wall's solidity and create a spot for stylised seafront decoration. The grapevine that will eventually drape the pergola has started its climb from a large pot. To stay healthy, it will need twice yearly feeding and topping up. Regular water is also essential.

OPPOSITE BELOW The entry steps with blue brachyscome and strappy yellow dietes repeats the colour scheme, then breaks all the rules with a pot of shocking pink geraniums alongside. The "window" is a mirror providing a spacious impression as it reflects the other side. A heavy wooden table and pergola add more village effect.

GROUND RULES

Potted herbs need regular feeding to keep them productive and will be pruned as they are harvested. Geraniums require twice-yearly feeding and topping up and need to be pruned back when straggly.

OPPOSITE ABOVE This simple and very functional deck provides two benefits. It gives level access from the house to a sloping area and provides space to catch winter sun. In the heat of summer two eucalypts filter the sun around the paving. The table and assorted pots of shade tolerant easy-care species make bright remarks among the green.

OPPOSITE BELOW A shed wall is almost enveloped in vines but a slice of light comes from a well-placed mirror. Green curvy cast-iron furniture sits elegantly among the arching fronds of aspidistra, clivia and strelitzia in matching tones. The Chinese elm displays its wondrous trunk and will drop its tiny leaves in autumn. However, its roots can be troublesome under paving. The shiny leaves of camellias reflect light, their winter flowers a bonus. New Guinea impatiens add zing.

ABOVE RIGHT The simple grey forms of the furniture continue the managed appearance of a neat and restful courtyard. Bands of well-maintained plantings include *Viburnum tinus*, gardenias, Australian native violet and clivia. Fine straps of mat rush dress the fountain. Golden robinia looks wonderful all year even when bare and twiggy in the winter sun. Potato vine gives density to the lattice screen.

out of the
summer heat

Walls and fences certainly wrap these three garden spaces. Most tiny gardens are similarly enclosed. But when dressed in vines and draped with boughs of screening trees you're hardly aware of enclosure at all. And thus, richly clad, they become cool and inviting retreats. Deciduous trees such as the golden robinia and Chinese elm will allow winter sun to penetrate when needed. See pages 118–119 for other useful small trees and pages 114–115 for climbers.

contemporary spaces

Garden styling can adapt to the demands of busy lives and modern taste for the uncluttered. Usually, it's a case of the simpler the better and quite often the most dramatically pared back plantings are the simplest. Maintenance required to keep the garden growing and under control is minimised. Furnishings can be anything from classic cane or linear teak, to sparklingly finished clean wood, shining modern metal or fifties retro. All are important in setting the scene. Remember however, it should never be cluttered.

BELOW Timber decking makes interesting patterns, an all-weather "stage" for entertaining and eliminates lawn maintenance. The retro furniture survives life outdoors and complements the stout stems of cordyline positioned at assorted heights. All the new shoots will leaf out, fully concealing the cut stems. At their feet are gazanias and purple-leafed tradescantia. A band of strappy mat rush connects grey and bold dracaenas with blue brachyscomes below.

OPPOSITE Simply elegant and elegantly simple, this space is leafed only with bamboo, its black canes making sharp vertical contrasts to the predominant horizontal lines. It will become a dense screen but has been well-contained in concrete to prevent its spread, bamboo's major weakness. It does need regular water, here provided by a watering system under the mulch. Lights give evening drama. White paving and pebble mulch enlarge the space while the mid-table succulent echoes the shining steel grey on the warm wood.

GROUND RULES

Sacred bamboo, cycads, flax, agaves and yuccas are all strong, upright forms that will provide bold architectural shape and structure to a contemporary garden style. All require minimal attention in the way of maintenance, feeding or water.

creative
courtyards

Creative courtyards are the result of assessing wisely how space is to be used, the surrounding conditions, and the owner's budget, in terms of both funds and time to spend on its establishment and maintenance. Following are some inspirational solutions. Some, with copious sun, like the one at left, are flowery extravaganzas. Many, being inner city spaces with contentious shade, are tonal themed hideaways or whimsical retreats.
Be realistic in assessment of your plot, inspired by our offerings and seek help from a designer if real problems appear.

urban paradise

This converted factory site had the loading dock maintained as garden space by the new front door. Clever design has kept the integrity of the site's original use while creating a secluded and lush inner city entry court. The original flooring remains with signs and markings of its early life but the walls have been fabulously painted. All the plantings are in generous pots. Heavy-duty reinforced steel joists are featured as the waterfall and a roller door is part of the screening wall. The clever use of a solid baffle immediately inside the entry gate provides some sound and sight seclusion.

BELOW The pool at the base of the fountain looks cool and supplies deliciously moist air to the ferns and ctenanthe that surround it. It's probably enough to keep the wall-mounted staghorns healthy but the other plants will require additional water. Weathered teak furniture turns as grey as the concrete floor while the purple paint adds its dramatic contrast.

OPPOSITE ABOVE LEFT The angled RSJ acts as the watershoot as it slopes from the supporting pillar of rocks. Industrial-strength pump and hose fittings maintain a generous and effectively cooling stream of water that falls into a pool big enough for a dip. Ferns and orchids revel in the moist air.

OPPOSITE ABOVE RIGHT An overview of the site displays the plan and abundant greenery, all planted in pots. A tall weeping fig against the brick wall contrasts well with the starbursts of dracaenas and the many-fingered succulent, *Euphorbia tirucalli*. A suspended, well-drained planter bed above the gate supports cycads, a sun tolerant climbing swamp fern, variegated bougainvillea and an orange-flowering crucifix orchid.

RIGHT The colourful terracotta wall paint and pots are echoed in some of the plantings, a strelitzia in the corner and the crucifix orchid on high. Other bright patches of colour come from begonias, impatiens and the variegated foliage of the succulent red bird flower, all happy in shade. Palms and a mother spleenwort, all richly green, demonstrate how well fed, watered and maintained they are in this semi-tropical garden.

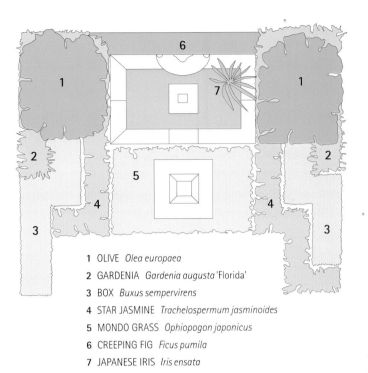

1 OLIVE *Olea europaea*
2 GARDENIA *Gardenia augusta* 'Florida'
3 BOX *Buxus sempervirens*
4 STAR JASMINE *Trachelospermum jasminoides*
5 MONDO GRASS *Ophiopogon japonicus*
6 CREEPING FIG *Ficus pumila*
7 JAPANESE IRIS *Iris ensata*

a beautiful
backdrop

Apartment gardens present specific problems. Most are above ground and must be provided with a waterproof base. The mix and weight of soil must comply with the engineering that supports it.

Here, the designer has used low, shallow-rooted and wind-resistant plants in the communal area above the garage. Palms are planted where roots can reach ground level. The private courtyard is paved and delineated with an orderly planting of clipped hedges surrounding a water feature. Free-form olives offer a soft contrast on either side. Paired pots of 'Sheena's Gold' duranta frame the view.

GROUND RULES

The minimum soil depth for any large plantings should be one metre, but this is not always possible, so check the depth before you plant. All areas, gardens and paving, must be well drained to prevent flooding of accommodation and drowning of plant roots. Drains must be checked and always clear.

a balinese hideaway

The tiny space pictured here has been dressed in cool-looking tropical greenery and delightfully detailed in an eastern theme. The exotic courtyard is ideal for summer living and serves equally well when weather dictates that it be viewed from the house. Most of these furnishings and features are Balinese and the flowers atop the figurines are a traditional Balinese practice. However, furnishings and souvenirs from any tropical holiday will transport you back there, when lovingly and authentically arranged amid lush greenery.

OPPOSITE ABOVE Varied sizes and species of palms growing in planter boxes and pots form the bulk of this greenery. Care must be taken in confined spaces not to select varieties with spikes in their stems. Tree ferns, small ferns, umbrellas of cyperus and leafy ctenanthe are all densely green. Colour is supplied only by the daily hibiscus offerings to the gods. Perfumed hoyas writhe from hanging baskets. The pergola could hold a bamboo blind if real shade were needed but is here trimmed with batik.

LEFT The cooling and relaxing effect of flowing water is just right here. The square tank is built from sleepers and lined with waterproof membrane. The mossy figure pouring water stands among fleshy-stemmed pickerel rush, callas and elephant ears, all perfect in shade and tolerant of splashing water.

RIGHT Positioned among banded palm stems, a pottery head on a plinth is decked, of course, with a hibiscus. Long stems of cyperus wave their windmill heads and flutter, even in light breezes. Streaked bromeliads, virtual epiphytes, grow well tucked into the dense shade at the base.

LEFT The owners planted the
narrow bed along the lattice with
a box hedge and on the decking
in front of it, a semicircular pond
was then constructed.
Waterproofed, painted a brilliant
blue, fitted with a pump and a
matching stand and urn, the
water gently overflows into the
cyperus-planted trough below.
The effect is calming and cooling.

completely contained

Two identically positioned and sized gardens in a multiple dwelling development have been styled by their owners. Both are completely contained by brick and lattice and both have a tiny serpentine garden built in the corner. But as these gardens are the private domain of the owners, individual tastes and garden dreams can be realised, while the landscaped communal area ties it all together (see pages 48 and 49).

OPPOSITE BELOW There's just room for a pretty and functional table and chairs. The glazed pot of strappy liriope teams with the other blue fixtures. A standard murraya in the corner bed and a duranta in the large terracotta pot, adorned with figures, frame the brick wall, as a creeping fig adds more greenery.

RIGHT Far less gardenesque, but just as restful, this rock and pebble design is almost Japanese in its simplicity. The sound and sight of water in the tiny pond, complete with fountain, works its liquid magic. Upright myrtle flag leaves contrast brilliantly with the round pebbles. The stone pillar is fitted with a speaker so the courtyard can be filled with sound, at a level, of course, that doesn't impinge on close neighbours!

GROUND RULES
In frost-free climates, most water plants will survive in water throughout the year and only require repotting every two years.

colour and romance

This romantically planted garden artfully uses tricks of colour and perspecitve to make the tiny space appear bigger than it really is. Light colours of paving, masses of white alyssum, urned petunias and climbing roses on the back wall expand the area. The central pathway makes the site seem longer, especially when the neat lonicera hedging angles inwards at the back as it leads to the circle of pond. The pond's roundness and the upright iris leaves that fill it are low enough to maintain the illusion. Permanent plantings with seasonal additions make this garden a year-round pleasure.

GROUND RULES

Fine light-coloured foliage, like the grey of the pines and silver pear, provides a background that appears to recede. Lower branches can be removed to reduce their bulk and increase the space around them. Anything large or dark-leafed would draw the background forward.

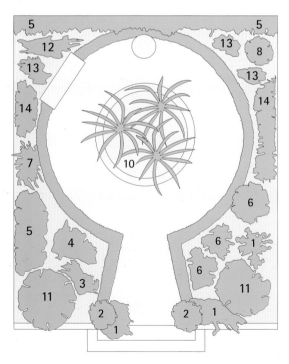

1 ALYSSUM
  Lobularia maritima
2 PETUNIA (WHITE)
  Petunia x hybrida

ROSES
3 *Rosa* 'Buff Beauty'
4 *Rosa* ' Souvenir de la Malmaison'
5 *Rosa* 'Iceberg' climbing
6 *Rosa* 'La Reine Victoria'

7 PINE
  Picea pungens 'Koster'
8 SILVER PEAR
  Pyrus salicifolia
9 LONICERA
  Lonicera nitida
10 YELLOW FLAG IRIS
   Iris pseudacorus
11 GOLD-LEAFED MOCK ORANGE
   Philadelphus coronarius 'Aureus'
12 COSMOS
   Cosmos bipinnatus
13 TREE POPPY
   Romneya coulteri
14 BAMBOO
   Fargesia nitida

Designed and maintained to act as vignettes of the larger natural landscapes of the countryside, most private Japanese gardens are, perforce, tiny. Viewed on entry and from the windows of the house, a new landscape in miniature is revealed by each window. Screening is achieved with fences and plantings are arranged in detail to paint the scenes. Moss and ground covers are used as grassy low growth, while rocks become mountains and pebbles become watercourses. Water receptacles in their various forms are a traditional and ceremonial inclusion. Traditional lanterns provide focal points.

OPPOSITE ABOVE Seasonal changes are marked by a gardenia for summer, and a camellia for winter/spring blooms, both sited beneath a Japanese maple which flames with colour in autumn. The understorey cover is a bamboo, *Sasa vietchii*, regularly clipped to keep it at this height. Formally arranged stepping stones lead through moss to the tsukubai – a stone water-bowl and replenishing bamboo pipe. The dipper, stones and bowl originate from tea ceremonies.

OPPOSITE BELOW A pebble "river" moves through "boulder" stepping stones beside the "reed-edge" of mini mondo grass. Beyond the picture, they join the main entrance path and curved clay wall, screening the enclosed garden. Aralias and ferns form "trees" in front of a bamboo frame for twining star jasmine. The lantern welcomes travellers.

RIGHT In designedly strict formality, seven bamboo stems surround a large mossy lantern. Note the irrepressible bamboo shoots emerging at the base of two of the stems, a constant with all bamboos in spring. Mondo grass edges the fence while low clipped dwarf bamboo forms a groundcover under the lantern.

GROUND RULES

Select non-invasive bamboo varieties or secure plants within root barriers. As long as spreading varieties are securely "caged" and the shoots in specific plantings like this are twisted off, you'll have no problems.

clever corners

Clever use of plants can take the sharpness out of a corner. They can be used to conceal eyesores, protect delicate treasures or blur the always-present boundaries that define neighbours' plots. It's always much easier if your borders meld, rather than stand defiant in their differences. Corners can be planted to become seasonal displays. A sasanqua camellia with anemones beneath, for example, provides delicate colour for autumn.

ABOVE In a beachside garden the endemic pandanus stands guard, deflecting the wind and filtering the sun over a less robust croton, the combination proudly shouting "tropics". More coastal survivors include the grey-leafed coast rosemary, strap-leafed mat rush and the almost ground-covering midgen berry, with its pink new foliage each spring. Ferns bulk out the gaps.

GROUND RULES

Ornamental grasses can be left to grow quite naturally, or can be cut back in early spring to 3cm above ground level, for neat new healthy growth.

RIGHT A paved area with defining brick walls is softened by pots. The plaited-trunks of a standardised weeping fig lift the leaf-top and allow nasturtiums to romp around its base, while the so-well-behaved climber 'Alice du Pont' mandevilla flowers madly. It only needs a warm wall to lean on and well-fed moist soil in order to perform like this each summer. Alyssum at its feet, violas and a chrysanthemum for autumn colour continue the bright display.

BELOW This corner is linked by subtle variations in tones, dictated by the dusty pink gate and paving. The accents come from strong variations in shapes. The pink of late summer plumes of variegated strappy miscanthus coordinates beautifully with the purple/pink tops of berberis which, after a bright autumn contrast, becomes a black twiggy form through winter. The mauve/grey spiked heads of the planum sea holly endure until pruned in spring.

shady solutions

If you're lucky enough to have a shady glade, make full use of it in the summer and drape it in cooling greenery. Select from the hundreds of shade-loving beauties avaialble to find the ones that do best in your site. Don't try to grow plants that need sun to keep them shapely and flowering – you'll only be disappointed. Take the lead from these gardeners and pave the area rather than struggle to grow a lawn. And when the weather cools, keep your courtyard looking great for viewing from the house.

OPPOSITE ABOVE Decorative paving makes a focus of the pool and metal fountain that is handsomely matched to the furniture. In this sub-tropical garden, there's a chance for a couple of hours of sun at the table, even in winter. Plantings are lushly evergreen – sacred bamboo, port wine magnolia, clipped lillypilly cone and fuchsia shelter under the deciduous jacaranda. Bright accents are provided by the lutchuensis camellia and grey germander.

OPPOSITE BELOW The courtyard here is potted and paved to create a low maintenance extension to the house. In summer, the family lives alfresco in the shade and, in winter, views the green screen from the sunny glassed room. The area is big enough for family projects, the washing, dining and entertaining large groups. The clever "shelf" gives plants more height and matching pots link the arrangement with the Asian motif.

RIGHT White painted furniture and abundant white alyssum leap from the dense greenery of ferns, palms, sacred bamboo, hydrangea and ivy. Sun is filtered by deciduous trees, both here and next door, so summers are shady and winters have sunlight through branches. The island bed demonstrates sad attempts at growing the wrong thing. Dense variegated ivy, ferns or fuchsias would be more successful.

making an entrance

The entrance, as the way in, should be
easy to find and well marked, but can
take many forms. It may, like this one,
be prettily dressed in seasonal colour
and patterns. It may be fenced and
secure, with just a hint of garden
exuberance tumbling over the wall.
It might even be a green and shady
glade or simply a collection of pots.
But whatever form it takes, let it make
a welcoming statement. You and your
guests will be pleased to be there.

community living

The benefits of pleasant planning and planting in community housing are many. Apart from providing beauty, these gardens can inspire a pride of place as well as tolerance between neighbours. Areas that are used by all – entrances, pathways to doors, access to garages and storage, for example – look most attractive and linked if an overall design and maintenance plan is established. While the garden shown here is the work of a landscape designer, committees, corporate bodies and some enjoyable teamwork can achieve equally pleasing results, with good community spirit enjoyed as a bonus.

BELOW The blue and white colour scheme of the tiled water feature on the rugged stone wall is echoed by the summer agapanthus reaching out of the front gardens. The deep green of their foliage and that of the box, topiary fig and gardenias remains constant and neat throughout the year to contrast with the exuberant golden robinias planted in the centre. Heavy troughs secured to the wall contain seasonal variations on the blue, white and yellow colour theme.

OPPOSITE ABOVE The upright form and green foliage of the sorbus contrasts with the generous abundance and reaching boughs of the golden robinia. Robinias adjust happily to pruning when sections grow into the pathway but are not happy in salty winds. The standardised gardenia, ornamental urn and potted vivid blue verbena are delightful details commonly only found in private gardens.

OPPOSITE BELOW LEFT In a terracotta feature pot the grass-like golden hakonechloa echoes the colouring of the robinias. Purple petunias repeat the agapanthus hues and can be seasonally changed with violas, primulas or alyssum. Succulents can also be useful and demand less upkeep. While decorative features in community areas need to be fairly robust, the pleasure they bring more than compensates for any upkeep they might require.

FAR RIGHT Curves constructed
for gardens reduce the linear
emphasis of pathways.

GROUND RULES

Neat clipping of figs and box
hedges calls for regular
maintenance or a resident
with time to contribute.
Watering systems ensure
plants stay alive and with a
slow-release fertiliser and an
annual soil refreshment
routine, they'll stay healthy.

OPPOSITE ABOVE Controlled neatness gives way to more natural grass and rock forms but all are linked by the remarkably stylised curve of lawn. Pebble mulch contrasts with black mondo grass but also acts to retain moisture and cool roots. Dwarf kangaroo paws will be dramatic for several months as will the wild tresses of *Poa labillardierei*. Neat propellor plants climb the steps.

OPPOSITE BELOW This Arizona planting copes with droughts and cold winters by using the plants from the local area. Green trunks are regional palo verdi with fine structured mesquite alongside. Sharply spiked large agaves are planted at the back while soft-tipped and ground-hugging varieties line the pathway edge. Grass clumps fill gaps, while extra drama is created by pots of succulents, paintwork and shadow-producing structures.

RIGHT A concrete river of pebbles in Burle Marx style meanders through a well-trimmed lawn. The effective cluster of "reeds" in the middle of the "river" is a very robust succulent, cheekily called mother-in-law's tongue. A group of coloured succulents decorates the step.

GROUND RULES

For dry-climate lawns, select hardy survivors, such as common couch or native grasses that adapt to mowing, and plant a tiny area to limit both water use and time spent on maintenance.

drylands entries

Dry but not dreary, these three gardens demonstrate pleasing arrangements for areas where rain is rare and water is precious. Rather than struggling with more demanding alternatives, the plants selected grow there naturally and are arranged with style. Dry area gardens can be modified with microclimates created by shade or a reticulated water feature to moisten the air. Features can also be made of other elements, like rocks, pebbles, sculptures or a shallow reflection pool. There is an ease and ruggedness in the garden that is other-than-lush.

stepping up

Steps are the safest and neatest method of coping with level changes in a garden, but they've other benefits as well. They can become a feature, a point of interest or a stage. They offer an enticing invitation to exploration, the changing levels suggesting a sunnier or shadier garden beyond the ultimate step. And as well as being a great place to sit, they also look lovely dressed in pots or lined with plants – fabulous potential for those with a tiny garden.

ABOVE Wide brick steps are given the formal treatment with a set of matching decorative urns planted with clipped balls of box. Behind is deciduous Virginia creeper for autumn colour and bare winter contrast.

LEFT Attractive rough stone steps invite us from deep shade to the brightness above. At the top, tomatoes and herbs relish the warm sun in contrast to the shade-loving ivy below.

OPPOSITE Paved front steps match the neat garden wall in this tiny entry, planted for year-round interest. Foaming gaura will flower through the warm months, till French lavender takes over for winter. Both are softly casual and need only an annual clipping at season-end. Standard white roses and crab apples add to the show while fragrant murrayas hedge the fence.

GROUND RULES

Box needs regular attention to maintain its neat shape. Virginia creeper also needs year-round clipping to curtail any errant growth.

outside the fence

OPPOSITE ABOVE A dangerous tree had to go, the buckled concrete was lifted and this sunny spot became a garden. Bricks give the site shape and retain the richly-manured additional soil. It now grows an exuberant collection of cumquat, roses, camellias, larkspurs, chalet and felicia daisies and purple creeping morning glory.

OPPOSITE BELOW This immaculate picket fence is a perfect foil for the street front spring show that stays neatly within its boundaries. The complementary colours of blue and yellow team brilliantly in ranunculi, anemones and violas. A neat white border of alyssum frills the edge. Both summer and winter annuals could carry on or alter the scene.

RIGHT With easy access for the gardener from the lawn in front, romping cottage splendour bursts over and through the fence. A white rose 'Lamarque', that flowers almost all year, clambers over a tree, chased by a small-flowered red 'Bloomfield Courage'. The red is repeated in the Flanders poppies and snapdragons in front. Yellow spires of *Wachendorfia thyrsiflora* and kniphofias clash raucously with pink wands of larkspurs and floppy clarkias. Parsley and yet-to-flower *Salvia forskaohlei* green up the border.

When your garden space is tight but there is room beyond your boundaries to spread, planting there makes good sense. Apart from these delightful overflows, other possibilities for garden extension could include railway edges, land abutting council property and community pathways. When such plantings are shared with neighbours, make sure you don't restrict their access to pathways or impede drivers' vision and that thorny branches or slippery debris won't become hazards. The edges of bushland should be strictly restricted to the growing of endemic species only to preserve plant colonies.

For drama and formal effect, it is better to use multiple plants of a single species rather than planting a great number of different plants.

LEFT In the back layer are tall stems of spring acanthus flowers. Their grey/green deeply cut leaves are a feature the rest of the year. Next, as a contrast, are smooth-edged 'Crowborough' lilies. They'll remain leafed all year if well watered and frost-free. Augusta gardenias circle the bed and the lighter green of a tiny box hedge scolds them into shape. The outside layer is mini-mondo grass. A central mound of *Helichrysum petiolare* re-introduces grey and is trimmed regularly.

OPPOSITE These layers almost roll into each other but are still clearly defined. Against the fence are *Tibouchina* 'Jules' which spot-flower in summer, becoming densely covered in autumn. A broad band of agapanthus stands next, in front of a casual clutch of Bangalow palms for contrast and height. Well-clipped sasanqua camellias fence the entry, murrayas define the path and box cubes punctuate the windows.

using layers

Serried rows of plants at ordained and well-maintained heights produce a wonderfully formal and dramatic effect. With the right selection of plant varieties – cultivars that naturally grow to about the right height, or plants that only grow slowly – maintenance is less of a chore. They won't require trimming every few weeks. Light regular trimmings however, will keep plants attractive all year. Contrasts of leaf colour and shape add another dimension.

the beauty of colour

The use of colour makes great impact at an entry, particularly when it's linked to the colouring of the house, the fence or gate, a feature or a tree. There's an art to using colour successfully. Complementary colours like blues and yellows or red and green have great impact, while tones of the same colour will blend and meld. Pale pastel hues can be grouped in any sort of combination and with any of the brights, while grey, white and bronze/black make useful contrasts or accents, lifting any arrangement. Year-round foliage colour, sometimes overlooked in planning, can be equally as useful as floral colour.

ABOVE Carmine valerian flowers tone with the rose inside the fence and the stems of the golden rose, 'Lady Hillingdon'.

OPPOSITE The informality of the winding path, edged with clumps of tonal plantings, gives impact to this detailed cottage. Grey lamb's ears on the left and grass (*Festuca glauca*) on the right match the path. The yellow of lady's mantle, euphorbia, calendula and wallflower echo the house paint, while the strong blue agapanthus complements all.

RIGHT Grey and yellow are teamed again, this time with smoky blue paintwork. Blue-grey cabbages, cerastium, festuca, *Artemesia* 'Powis Castle' and *Senecio* 'Silver Dust ' sit amongst yellow kangaroo paws, cabbage flowers, sedum, violas, coreopsis and constrasting purple pansies, white daisy clumps and pale trails of *Convolulus* 'White Gladdy'. Red salvias add a bright dash.

clean and clipped

Clipped and shaped hedges and features were once the preserve of large estates with a team of artisans to maintain order. In small sites, however, it takes very little time to shape and neaten a hedge or topiary and thus provide the order and balance that is so fitting in a tiny design.

BELOW This sun-drenched terrace features drought-tolerant plantings of varied leaf form and colour, rounded into symmetrical shapes. *Pittosporum tobira*, and 'Petite Salmon' oleander frame the window – the flowers of the oleander will match the wall colour. Below, mounds of prostrate rosemary cascade - a pair of them revealing the ledge that supports them. Round of lavender cotton share the front with rosemary and a white iberis.

OPPOSITE ABOVE A tiny front entrance is simply but brilliantly laid out. The back wall, a hedge of compact *Hebe* 'Autumn Glory', sets the colour scheme. Spot flowers appear throughout summer with a major flush in autumn. Beneath are autumn-flowering zephyranthes and purple lobelia, while mondo grass fills the gaps in the entrance stepping-stones. Well-shaped figs in pots on the verandah continue the formality, softened by a toning pot of the same lobelia and pretty pink petunias.

OPPOSITE BELOW This angle reveals just how small the garden is and shows a neat link of assorted paving. Clipped lonicera holds a bank of diosma that will flower mauve/pink in winter. The sasanqua camellia hedge is less rigid but screens the fence nicely.

GROUND RULES

Slow-growing and small-leafed specimens such as box, rosemary, lavender cotton, conifers, figs lavender and camellias are often used for hedging and clipping as they only need trimming two or three times a year. It's best to be regular and to clip after growth spurts or flowering. Fast-growers need more regular trimming. Bloomers, such as daisies and roses, require regular dead-heading and trimming back to a new growth point to keep them in bloom. Avoid heavy pruning and resultant displays of sticks. Some plants, such as diosma, won't shoot from woody growth.

OPPOSITE Brightly painted furniture is scaled small to fit the area but is still functional. The big pots are essential for the large figs and the tree shaping allows access and doesn't crowd the tiny area. Half pots are another alternative. The terracotta disc and driftwood treasure are elegantly decorative and the generous planter on the ledge contrasts with the green of its abundant ivy geranium growth.

ABOVE Mixed lobelia tumble from a window box in a tiny sunlit garden where Spanish lavender and 'Hidcote Pink' penstemon fill the gap between the house wall and picket fence.

the smallest space

Often just corners where dead leaves and and bits of paper are blown, very small spaces can be dressed, not to kill, but to look pleasing. Scale furniture to fit the site or simply place a shelf or stand that can hold a pot or parcels as you search for the key. Plants hanging from, or growing up, a wall utilise vertical space. Floor level corner pots, a simple shelf with garden ornaments or a window box make use of horizontal surfaces and can brighten up a bleak area. When the space is small, less is best – but nothing's no go at all.

going around
the side

It may be narrow, it may be shady or a wind-
tunnel but it's probably vital access from one
area to another. Sometimes it's an all-important
entry. Or it may just be the unloved and unused
gap between fences and houses that presents
so dispiriting a view from inside. If faced with
such an area, let your imagination soar with the
inspired treatments on these pages and turn
the site into a sight to delight in. This paradise,
here, is right against a wall. Wide pavers curved
around a bromeliad-draped tree are under-
planted with tropical-looking shrubs and pots.

LEFT Assorted types and sizes of palms set the scene while Madonna lilies, aspidistras and tropical eucharist lilies act as groundcovers in the shade with variegated liriope in the centre. All softly drape the edges. Aglaenemas and a purple-leafed philadendron erupt from the liriope "lawn" and impatiens flower in the sun-dappled back.

BELOW Casual stone steps are densely and lovingly planted with soft, tumbling shade-happy edgings in this temperate zone garden. Mountain violets, parochetus, campanulas, club moss, acantholinum, cyananthus and baby's tears creep about. Above the steps stand English daisies, corydalis, aquilegias, dicentras and hostas, among the abundant plantings.

softening the edges

There are gardens where neatly clipped edges are essential to the effect. But these three show more casual elements where the gardens just grow and the effect is soft and yielding. They also demonstrate the generosity of nature and how gardeners with limited space just can't resist planting more. However it is important to keep much-used pathways clear. Overhangs can be bothersome when you're carrying things or when it's wet, and in the under storey, plants with sharp spikes or slippery debris can cause accidents.

RIGHT A straight brick path has its business-like demeanour adjusted by flouncing beauties along its edge. Cerise lychnis, forget-me-not and pink aquilegia start the tactics on the left. They'll all re-seed for next year. 'Red Chief' alstoemeria flaunts through summer, dies back for winter and reshoots in spring. On the right is always-flowering French lavender that needs a trim in late summer. A geranium with handsome leaves, a mini white daisy and an *Anemone blanda* clump display less wildness.

LEFT A neat shaping of the rosemary hedge against the house demands a clip three or four times a year. This means minimal lengths are removed to keep it in shape and no hard woody ends are revealed. By way of contrast on the other side of the path, lolling penstemon and reaching cleomes exuberantly repeat the colour of the house and paving.

hedging the edging

OPPOSITE BELOW In a hot, dry sheltered position with brick paving, the hedging is random. Lime-green shrubby euphorbia, crassulas and the great felty-leafed *Kalanchoe beharensis* roam tall with accents of limestone, alyssum and succulents at their feet. Euphorbia and alyssum will seed and replace themselves generously. Only the "dead carcasses" have to be removed and errant seedlings repositioned or removed.

RIGHT Ivy clings to the struts of a metal fence, sealing and disguising it. It is trained and kept trim by redirecting or removing its wandering stems. Shaped sentinels of variegated box make an orderly line at the base and are separated from the lower all-green box edging by straps of mondo grass. Both the box borders will need clipping twice or three times annually. The streaked grass is variegated liriope.

GROUND RULES

Climbers which will spread horizontally as well as vertically, such as ivy, Boston ivy, akebia, hardenbergia and tecoma, are all ideal choices for wall covers.

The style and the size of your hedging depends on how much space you have to fill. Neat and slim upright forms such as sacred bamboo, palms or bamboo can form casual thin edging. Wider areas allow robust but casual hedging, like the scene at bottom left. Orderly shaping in a similar sized area gives a crisp and formal effect. And when space is very tight, a fence clothed with a wall of vines and a march of trimmed forms in front makes it easy to be green. In all cases, it's the consistent treatment that creates the impact.

a festival of flowers

Paths winding through flowers can supply both an overall visual feast as well as a chance to savour individual highlights – shape, colour, texture and perfume – as the path is wandered. In some climates, the festival can keep performing right through the year with seasonal splendours ringing in the changes. By mixing self-seeding annuals, bulbs and perennials, the show will go on, but remember that such plantings require a lot of maintenance.

BELOW Here, early summer delights include perennials, orange oriental poppy and carmine valerian, self-seeding purple and white aquilegias and candytuft with flowering bulbs of allium, Peruvian scillas and alstoemarias. They all meld together and flow into the mutabilis and carmine roses at the back.

OPPOSITE ABOVE An orderly but still festive arrangement with an orange/red bulb clump *Cyrtanthus brachyscyphus* carrying the colour of a rose like 'Just Joey' or 'Royal Dane'. The ground is wreathed in white alyssum, purple/blue prunella, violas, clumps of pinks and sweeps of thyme.

OPPOSITE BELOW This festival of pastel tonings lights the way to the gate. Yellows and creams come from annual petunias, violas, Californian poppies and bright coreopsis, perennial sisyrinchium and a climbing blushed rose on the roof. Pink clusters along the edge are perennial dianthus with rich heads of patio roses behind. The white shrub-like plant on the right is the fast-growing annual lavateria, with a splash on the left from a white nicotiana. Lime colouring comes from another nicotiana and euphorbia. Lamb's ears and artemesia provide grey highlights.

stepping stones

Both practical and decorative, stepping stones allow you to move easily about the garden. They don't require elaborate construction, can simply be repositioned if the need arises, provide access along garden spaces for maintenance work or detailed viewing and they can be dressed in plants. Make sure they're steady to the footfall and won't be slippery when wet. Stone, brick sets or concrete slabs serve the purpose.

OPPOSITE ABOVE These delightfully decorative fish mosaic slabs, winding their way through a colourful garden patch, were made by the owner. The mondo grass that surrounds them allows sunlight into an otherwise densely-planted bed. The colour arrangement is set to yellow and cream from violas, kangaroo paw, a sedum and cabbage flowers, grey from cabbage leaves and sempervivum, and mauve/purple from ajuga and petunias. A daisy adds a little dash.

OPPOSITE BELOW Here the scene is woodsy and muted, with stones set amidst purple-leafed ajuga, clumps of white dianthus, white annual poppies and a chalet daisy, all of which fit well among deep green gardenia and generous acanthus leaves.

RIGHT These stone steps, inserted into the slope, allow the walker to climb a rise. The dense plantings not only dress the scene but also hold the soil in place as well. Both ajugas, the purple is 'Atropurpurea' and the variegated is 'Multicolor' (not very pink in this shade). 'Zanadu' philadendron reaches in from the left.

the well-used path

Paths, while practical and providing essential access, needn't be dreary. Turning the prosaic into the poetic can be achieved in many ways. A bend can reduce a path's linear rigidity, whether introduced by plantings or by an arrangement of pots. A bleak end can be transformed with paint, a spectacular pot, an ornament or a trim on the door or wall surface. A feature at the end provides real emphasis and a focus.

BELOW The architecture implies the Iberian theme that this designer has enhanced romantically with plantings and ornaments – even a stylised shed. Random flagstones have gravel inserts with occasional mini mondo and ajuga tufts. In the sun, well-mulched restrained plantings suggest arid conditions, with lantana and a potted begonia boldly exuberant beside a more sober gardenia. Straps of clivea, mondo, and dietes shelter in the shade of a *Michelia champaca*, with a bright accent – broom or perhaps hypericum – potted at the end of the path.

OPPOSITE ABOVE The straight and narrow of this path is relieved by a seating bay with pots of mini morning glory and the box-lined entry opposite. The rest heads purposefully to the pretty gate with light lamb's ears to guide the way. Dark green box and gardenias grow at the base of clusters of birch.

GROUND RULES

Make sure the walking surface can cope with the hard wear and not become puddles in the wet. If one surface treatment is not possible along the full length of path, link different surfaces with gravel or groundcovers, which will help to unite them.

RIGHT These interesting old walls have their own impact so heading through them for the door and the sunny courtyard is a pleasure. Even though it's narrow, the path has been dog-legged around a coral tree with its red winter flowers. Growing beneath it are crassulas, a red kalanchoe, sedums and a grey succulent senecio, with tall aloes towards the door. The soft groundcover is *Cymbalaria muralis.* In the sun, a rangy geranium occupies a stunning pot, with a streaked spiky agave alongside.

gardens of
seclusion

When seeking seclusion, the aim is to
keep out what's outside – be it people,
traffic, noise, an ugly view or wind.
What's needed is a barrier. This chapter
features some clever techniques, such
as the solid stone wall pictured here,
with an abundant private garden
sheltering in its lee. Whatever you use,
make sure that the seclusion you create
becomes an area in which it's
a pleasure to be secure.

LEFT A slatted bamboo fence is a relatively fragile barrier, but when it's bulked up with vines it shows new strengths. This fence is appealingly twined with the large ruffled leaves of Chinese gooseberry. If you're after fruit, you need to plant a male and a female. Being deciduous, they will leave the barrier twined but not leafed in winter. A nasturtium takes advantage of the leg up and a rose, 'Wedding Day', casually meanders through.

OPPOSITE A surround of grassy leaves frames and protects a verdigris-toned Pan and his pool. Movement of the leaves provides a delightful contrast to the still beauty of the statue. On the left, gaura and a smoke bush soften the edges in front of the New Zealand flax and draping *Miscanthus floridulus* screen. Subtle splodges of colour from dietes, geranium and purple orach are reinforced by nicotiana, *Anthemis* 'A.C. Buxton' and a snapdragon in bright mode.

foliage screens

A "green" screen can be just as effective as a solid wall and has other benefits as well. It is far more effective a barrier when screening wind, because it breaks the flow instead of forcing it to hurtle vengefully over the top. It offers ever-changing delights as plants grow and respond to the change of seasons. And it's rarely motionless – be it breezes or wildlife appreciating the protection, you'll always be aware that it's a living screen.

1 CAST-IRON PLANT *Aspidistra elatior*
2 WATER FERN *Azolla caroliniana*
3 TRAILING FERN *Columnea microphylla*
4 WATER IRIS *Iris* cv

5 GARDENIA *Gardenia augusta* 'Florida'
6 MOP-HEAD HYDRANGEA *Hydrangea macrophylla*
7 CRAB APPLE *Malus* cv
8 STAR JASMINE *Trachelospermum jasminoides*

reducing the height

This great sheet of privacy-wall would have overpowered the pathway and presented a starkly bright view from the house, but five clever techniques have been used and combined with flair to solve the problem. Using any one of these ideas will help disguise a featureless expanse. In the foreground, a narrow planter trough built up against the wall provides a second level of greenery, visually cutting the wall in half. The fountains and water trough below the raised garden create a diverting feature, producing soft trickling sounds to echo in the area. A vine-clad arch breaks up the next expanse of wall and, with its seat positioned for eventual shade, is given real purpose. Pots, raised to an eye-catching height on solid pillars, also provide a visual break from the wall's mass and standardised trees, beside and beyond the arch, add yet another level of greenery.

a sense of security

There are as many terms to describe a sense of security as there are ways of providing it. Garden walls with intercom-controlled entry, solid fences with lockable gates, wooden fences with extended tops, metal fences, brush fences and walls of stacked stones – all are distinctly solid and impenetrable. Another form of fencing provides security just by implying it. Boundaries are marked and the way is blocked, but the screen is open enough to allow vision through it. Lattice, wood or bamboo slatted screens and louvred pales can all be used for this more enticing, less fortified effect.

OPPOSITE ABOVE The sunny side of the house, ideal for drying clothes, is often the front or entrance area and a screen from this prosaic chore may be called for. The choice made by the owners here is an attractive example – a three-part fence that supplies sufficient room and air in the sunny court. Such a solid screen can also be used to effectively hide garbage and recycling bins. The prolific vine that refuses to be hidden is *Myoporum parvifolium*.

OPPOSITE BELOW The detailing of this painted lattice fence and entry with entwining star jasmine provides a boundary that is secure without being heavy or solid. It effectively cuts off the garden from the car access area, enclosing a safe site for children or pets while adding an attractive garden feature.

RIGHT A solid brush fence of good height shields the house perfectly while the twisting path directs the eye casually but invitingly to its entry. The slatted bamboo screen at the end directs the visitor to turn right but also provides a tempting glimpse of what lies ahead.

links with lattice

Lattice can provide a useful screen in the garden. Allowing glimpses from both sides, as well as penetrating breezes, it is nonetheless solid enough to use in supported construction of walls or gates. Like any milled timber in the garden, it has a limited life, but the use of quality treated lattice and/or regular painting will add longevity, as will frames surrounding the lattice. So too will selecting vines like mandevilla, Australian sarsaparilla, Natal ivy or muehlenbeckia, that don't develop thick stems to break the lattice as they expand .

OPPOSITE ABOVE A tropical paradise to relish in the winter has been created on the sun-baked side of this house. The lattice wall screens the car and bin storage, effectively excluding them from the tropical oasis. 'Lady Di' pandorea climbs the lattice and pillars of a striking cordyline cultivar provide a vivid contrast at the base. Iris line the feature pool, while more accents are provided by bromeliads, impatiens and variegated marantas, among the greenery of palms, ferns, clivea, mondo grass and vireyas.

LEFT A decorative gate and fence at the side of this garden is sturdy enough to keep the children and pets enclosed while prettily dressed in shade-loving species. We get a tantalising peep through the partition which is clothed with potato vine on top and Canary Island ivy. Hydrangeas, lilies, variegated iris and mondo grass form matching pedestals for a pair of trees, while an azalea catches a shaft of sunlight.

RIGHT Lattice as artwork? It's certainly an important design detail in this herb-filled garden. Richly painted, the lattice panel forms a wonderful foil to the purple of the 'Victoria' salvia and golden oregano, threaded through with spires of tarragon. The lattice also provides sufficient screen to blur the images of the water feature on the other side.

points of
interest

A focal point, a feature or a declared interest, proudly displayed, can give even the tiniest garden that extra something that makes it distinctly personal. Let your choice reveal your point of view, your sense of style or your dreams – as this fountain Cupid does so gently here.

ABOVE LEFT This zany potted display has tonal bands in front with purples and pinks of osteospermum and *Kalanchoe pumila*, contrasted by yellow violas, snapdragons and calendulas. Assorted lush greenery circles behind, including a variegated fig and a Japanese maple in new pink foliage dressed with a fluttering doll.

ABOVE RIGHT Deliciously simple and rustic, a terracotta urn is set amongst yellow wallflowers and cradled by mauve-toned violas and chive flowers. A stem of lily stands tall behind.

BELOW LEFT These large and strongly designed pots make a feature of their form and their plantings. The tiny winter blooms of lutchuensis camellia are scented and its growth is a wayward contrast to the clipped box forms beside it – the Japanese variety showing winter colour while the English box remains green. Other contrasts are provided by the spontaneous impatiens growing at the base of one pot and the burst of alyssum behind.

BELOW RIGHT Fabulous wall colour and a groomed gravel floor set the scene for an arrangement of cacti. Drama comes from using a contrast of forms, such as the dumpy golden barrel and pillars of silver torch in pots, with rosettes of spiny agaves in the gravel. A collection like this is best kept under cover to prevent damage from hail and very wet conditions.

the flexibility of pots

Let me count their ways. Individually, pots are ornamental, whether filled with a foam of plants, dedicated to an architectural plant in isolation, or even left unfilled. They can be arranged in random romantic clusters or follow a formal plan of strictly regimented rows. They can house a sea of greenery, or a swathe of colour. They will add highlights and contrasts to a garden display. And they can be moved to chase the sun or shade, or into a feature position when the plants they house are at their best.

CLOCKWISE FROM TOP LEFT
Spring delights of tulips and
toned violas make a colourful
seasonal statement.
In a sea of vibrant red and white
romping petunias, lobelia,
primula, salvia and impatiens,
stands a brilliant contrast bowl,
subtly aswim with water fern and
mini papyrus.
Iris grow in the water~trough,
while on the rim stand pots of
compact roses, geranium, sedum
and seedling petunias for later in
the season.
Boxed box with a bird, for a focal
point of elegant simplicity.
Here a collection of treasures
surrounds a pony tail palm.
A shallow dish of grey gravel,
golden sedum and assorted
sculptural echeveria.
To keep a cloud of petunias in
shape, select compact varieties
and pick them frequently; they're
great in tiny vases.
Round succulents look good in
square pots while petunias
trumpet their own success.

ABOVE LEFT Siting a matching nasturtium next to a similarly painted seat is good planning, but the happy accident is when the leaves wind through, their round shape making a bold statement against the angular wood.

ABOVE RIGHT A painted but weathered seat and a zinc café table rest appropriately in a garden made abundant by spring. Roses and star jasmine scent the air, while silver-leaved olive and tanacetum provide contrasts to the romping white and blue forget-me-nots, seaside daisies and true geraniums below – a perfect outlook for the lucky tenants of the bird-house!

CENTRE This handmade stone bench is sited with a bamboo and lime phygelius screen. Festoons of climbing 'Iceberg' roses team with a romneya, cosmos and potted petunias. Thyme and mint await the gentle trampling of feet.

peaceful places to sit

The structure of a seat in the garden can be highly ornamental, whether it's large or small, antique, modern, derivative, homemade or not even functional. It serves its purpose in that it sets a scene. And if it is peaceful, has an outlook, is conveniently positioned and is comfortable, it can become a favoured site for a bit of a rest, a spot for a drink or a personal retreat. This random collection demonstrates just some of these pleasures.

OPPOSITE BELOW LEFT Among the richly patterned foliage of tree paeony, golden hop vine and meconopsis rests a battered café chair holding a platter of bulbs, once positioned to meet the sun, now well past their spring prime.

OPPOSITE BELOW RIGHT This greyed seat against a Tuscan-toned wall is set for autumn with a standard sasanqua camellia, wind flowers, bright impatiens and Australian native violet scrambling underfoot. The echeveria in the urn tones well.

RIGHT ABOVE In this floral bower the wooden seat is backed by blue/grey plectranthus and artemesia. A crown of jasmine and arms of a 'Cecile Brunner' rose arch above. In the foreground, mauve alliums, salvia and geranium mound up behind golden feverfew and oregano.

RIGHT BELOW This seat turns the tree into a desirable feature and the corner into a useable space. Tree trunks move, so space must be left when fitting the seat, and the roots need air and water so the pavers are placed on sand. The water feature adds strength and the unusual fencing ensures complete privacy.

accent plants

Some plants have a really dramatic form. They may not be pretty or particularly well-flowered, and they usually don't have significant seasonal changes. They just look good all year, adding reliable structure to a garden and are thus the so-called architectural plants. They make a statement purely because of their shape, their leaves, their colouring or their size. Some make an impact by combining a couple of these features but others exhibit one feature alone. And because they are so dramatic, they are often best used on their own.

FAR LEFT Black cane bamboo is used alone in this elegantly formal courtyard. The stems look dramatic against the wall of green and the light fluttering leaves make a bright contrast. New stems will emerge green, but darken with age. (See pages 26 and 41 for care of bamboo.)

CENTRE LEFT The texture of clustered echeveria makes a nice contrast with the hard flat rocks and bouncy cushion of thyme. In this situation, shape, rather than colour, provides the foil of each to the other.

BELOW The sinuous figure is cleverly paired with the curving forms of her grass encirclement, a green miscanthus. Even the plumes echo the angle of her bent arms and the almost constant movement of the grass acts as both a contrast and a fabulous accent.

ABOVE RIGHT Grass trees can stand alone as an exclamation point or be grouped together for a statement of significance.

CENTRE LEFT Fabulous rosetted agaves make dramatic feature plants in all but very frosty climate zones, but most are armed with sharp and hazardous spikes. This form, *Agave attenuata* is not barbed, so it is safe for pathside planting.

CENTRE RIGHT Always tops for drama in a mild climate shade, bromeliads look great all year. Some, like this neoregalia, flush red for even greater impact during summer.

BELOW RIGHT Included in this scene are three varieties of dracaena and the broader rubra cordyline. The drama comes from the similarities in the massed varieties, making a great tropical impact. Differences appear in their colour and form but they all have strap-like leaves.

ABOVE LEFT Formal simplicity with a sweep of stone steps and a ceramic sphere positioned on a dark-toned bed of pebbles. The contrasts of colour and forms here are dramatic.

ABOVE RIGHT A mosaic patterned plinth holds aloft a glass lotus form in wonderfully lush hues. The trickles of water and the broad-leafed heliconias complete the delightfully tropical effect.

CENTRE LEFT A classical head, weathered by "antiquity" peers imperiously through wisteria in summer greenery. Majestic in all seasons, in winter he can gaze without interruption.

CENTRE RIGHT A sandstone wall, espaliered fruit and recycled aggregate paving set the stage for this carved stone fish.

BELOW LEFT Carved in lifelike poses and painted in a similar manner, a family of magpies has set up home on poles in this garden, above a lawn of knotweed. Their head heights are as varied as the waving flumes of the miscanthus behind.

BELOW RIGHT Instead of being positioned in bold isolation, this charming cherub on her sphere crouches diffidently amongst a protective bed of sea holly.

ABOVE A moss encrusted
Balinese god pours a trickle of
water into a pond filled with
pickerel rush and cyperus in this
tropical courtyard. The hibiscus
adornment is a Balinese tradition.

RIGHT This squatting lad and his
captured fish are positioned so
the fountain maintains a clear
circle in the duckweed in front.
Behind stand Louisiana iris,
gorgeous in bloom during spring,
while the strap-like leaves look
dramatic all year. The mirror gives
extra depth to the scene.

garden art

Even in a tiny garden there's room for garden art, be it in a pond,
sequestered in a garden corner, prominent on a pathway or positioned
on a wall. As shown here, a piece of sculpture is a popular choice, but
equally alluring are mosaic work, suspended structures and wind or
power driven installations. For all art in the garden, the only provisos
are that the work is weatherproof and has sufficient space around it
to make its full impact.

survivors in dry conditions

Where the sun beats down and there's not much water to splash about in, it's wise to dress appropriately. The same applies to the garden. Deck it with plants that happily tolerate the conditions and they'll look good year round. A stressed plant is a miserable sight and a miserable garden quickly becomes dispiriting. Most Australian, Mexican and Mediterranean native plants, and species, such as succulents and cacti, that originate in deserts, offer a rich palette of suitable material. See also pages 50 and 51.

CLOCKWISE FROM BELOW LEFT Swaying grass clumps, (endemic varieties will be most reliable) repeat the shapes of the cabbage tree palms above them, while lavender, a purple lampranthus and a doryanthes complete the mix; massed annual paper daisies, such as 'Bright Bikini', remain gloriously floriferous through summer and autumn; clipped westringia, trimmed austromyrtus edging, grevilleas pinched back to keep them low and a pair of standardised *Eucalyptus globulus 'Compacta'* show Aussie natives in distinctly gardenesque style.

ABOVE LEFT Mass plantings of different colour species are used to create swirls of pattern in a dramatic display of low succulents with accents of tall yuccas.

ABOVE RIGHT An informal corner is created here by a shrubby wattle, mallee eucalypt and a selection of low pink-flowering shrubs with grass-like clumps. Plants like this, clustered about a rock in a mulch of leaf litter, create a natural bush scene and a very hardy garden.

CENTRE LEFT An ancient grass tree stands tall in a drylands garden of gazanias, pig face and osteospermums. The grey shrub at the back is Flinders Range wattle.

CENTRE RIGHT A baked scree border is perfect for Sturts desert pea, a Swan River daisy and a gold dust wattle, at the top.

BELOW Torches of banksia, straps of lomandra, sculptural folds of homoranthus and a grass tree with developing flower-spike show the variety of forms that can be combined so effectively and thrive in rugged conditions.

LEFT A gorgeously flower-filled garden like this needs a shed to store garden gear and supplies. Here the owners have concealed the shed and made it melt into the surrounding garden by wrapping it in a parthenocissus vine, and completed the scene with a dovecote. Hydrangeas, fuchsias, hellebores and impatiens draw attention forward.

CENTRE LEFT Passionfruit, shown here, do well in subtropical zones, kiwi fruit thrive in temperate areas and grapes will survive most climates. If you're after a productive vine, all are attractive and the latter two are deciduous.

CENTRE RIGHT Variegated and plain ivy on the fence, with roses and bougainvillea clambering up the house provide a lot of colour and interest as they clothe the vertical space in a tiny area.

BELOW FAR LEFT A motley wall has been concealed by espaliered shrubs and the length of the narrow passage is disguised by the use of three rose-clad arches. Lavender and herbs enjoy the sun-baked strip on the left while hydrangeas and camellias nestle on the shady side.

climbing for cover

OPPOSITE BELOW (TOP RIGHT)
Cleverly clad in creeping fig, the
barbecue no longer dominates
this small courtyard.

OPPOSITE BELOW (BOTTOM RIGHT)
A brilliantly painted wall is
patterned with a mock espalier
of star jasmine trained up a wire
frame. In front, salvia of the same
shade as the wall will flower
through summer, while the
hellebores starred all winter.
The pillars of the pergola are
wrapped in Virginia creeper.

RIGHT This fine old grape has
developed a sizeable trunk and
the dense shade that was here
through summer is significantly
reduced by the falling autumn-
toned leaves. In winter the patio
becomes a delightful sun-trap.
By pruning back to the major
"branches" each winter, the new
spring growth completely covers
the area by summer.

Vines are delightful in any garden especially when they dress a wall,
conceal an outrage, link plantings and provide summer shade. In small
gardens they are really to be treasured as they provide all these
benefits as well as a chance of extra flowers, green cover, autumn
colour and even fruit. Better still, they grow above ground or on
vertical surfaces, taking up minimal extra room. When space is limited
it's great to use a deciduous vine that will create two different
environments in the same area – a shaded summer retreat when in
leaf and a sun-bathed winter arena when bare.

ABOVE LEFT Stems of sealing wax palm back this deep, square pool where fish, water lilies, water lettuce and pickerel rush thrive. Watching fish is a relaxing and contemplative pursuit.

ABOVE RIGHT Michelia and rocks conceal the pump and pipe of a tsububai, while the catchment area of pebbles supports both the bowl and water iris in this small Japanese water feature with decorative stone lantern.

CENTRE A natural-looking pond, fed by a trickle over rocks, fills half the courtyard. Mondo grass, dwarf sacred bamboo and palms, flanked by a small-leafed camellia keep the scene in scale.

BELOW Composition-stone spheres, one gurgling water, are arranged in a bed of pebbles beside a patterned path. The palm and wet gloss soften the edges.

water features

The sound and sight of water in a garden provide many charming benefits. The sounds of moving water produce a soothing effect and help to mask ambient sounds of traffic, voices or echoing footsteps. When circulated by a pump, the water remains clear, insect-free, and oxygenated for plants and fish. Easiest to install are simple pools of water that reflect the sky and surrounding plants, patterns of wind or rain and the glossy sheen of wetness – such as a dish of water or a birdbath. More complex fixtures need more space – and a bigger budget.

CLOCKWISE FROM RIGHT A ceramic urn overflows into a neatly maintained lily pond with fish. Murraya, box and viburnum add greenery to the scene.

A grotto fountain and pond along a pathway are dressed with small-leafed camellias and yellow flag iris. Grape ivy clambers aloft with the young acrobats.

The detailing on this sculpted birdbath, along with the sky's limpid reflection on the water and the lichen encrustation on the rock, make it a tiny gem in this garden. Keep water bowls reliably full to ensure a constant stream of flying visitors.

Slabs of stepping stones, bridges and still water make bold contrast with pebbles and plantings. In the "river" are water iris and lilies, while acornus, mondo grass, Japanese maple, a well-shaped pine and a decorative lantern adorn the banks.

Simplicity itself – set among sedums, an old copper preserving pan is filled with pebbles and enough water to gloss them.

The elegant purity of this pond's designed lines is softened by the flow of water, the random arrangement of pebbles and the floating water lettuce and lilies.

ABOVE LEFT The lion's head fountain against a bagged and moulded wall is illuminated from below at night with a spotlight in the pool. By day the sun lights it from above.

ABOVE RIGHT The candle, securely encased in a lantern is not disturbed by rain or wind and is no threat to the kangaroo paws that reach toward it.

CENTRE Special effects for a special event – tall candlesticks and low candles light the way across the flower strewn lawn while paired candelabra and fairy lights in the figs highlight the door. Care is needed to protect flowing fabrics and happy guests.

BELOW LEFT Lighting on the beautiful trunks of silver birch just picks up the silent figure seated below. In the eerie light, the boy and his water bowl seem almost phantasmal.

BELOW RIGHT A heavy-based candlestick, topped with a stout candle and arranged against a cleared wall, demonstrates safe yet romantic lighting.

ABOVE LEFT Down-lights, placed at regular intervals, clearly mark the way on a flight of steps. From the point of view of safety, they make enormous sense, but the bonus is the illumination of the delightful stonework in the wall.

ABOVE RIGHT A "classic" bronze bust has been positioned on a wooden plinth to lift it clear of the encircling fuchsias. Spot-lit from below, it emerges benignly at night. The undersides of the leaves too, produce different patterns to the scene by day.

adding some light

Until quite recently, garden lighting, with wiring fitted by an electrician, has been the only practical means of guiding guests to the entry in the dark. Now, do-it-yourself safe systems with assorted light fittings and wiring that can be plugged in as needed give owners an opportunity to create dramatic feature points and new vistas in their gardens at night. There are even specialist nightscape designers. Take care when positioning candles or any naked flame in the garden as leaves desiccate in the heat and quickly ignite.

in the shade

Shade in the garden is a delight – cool, restful and dappled with changing patterns. A shady garden usually means you've got trees producing a canopy either in your own garden or nearby, providing a continually changing backdrop and adding interest as they entice local wildlife. Buildings also produce shade. When planning for your shade garden, assess shade patterns through the day, both summer and winter, then select plants that do well in these conditions – your local nursery can advise. White or cream variegated foliage and shiny leaves will add brightness. See also pages 44–45 for shady solutions.

BELOW In dappled light under a high leafy shrub, acanthus thrives, its spring flowering spires emerging from attractive, broad well-patterned leaves. If kept watered and snail-free, they're attractive all year. In front are winter-deciduous, blue-leafed hostas that need the same care – this is a perfect position for them both. *Salvia guarantica*, on the left, will cope with some shade.

ABOVE LEFT Wisely, durable paving and deck surface this shady corner, instead of struggling grass. Leafy shapes of soft tree fern, bird's-nest fern and small palm varieties gleam from the shade while spotted leopard plant lights up an edge.

ABOVE RIGHT Palms of assorted height create this green jungle scene, surrounded by orchids, bromeliads and elkhorn. The figure on a rock above a pool near a bird's-nest fern, and a birdbath by the path provide decorative highlights.

CENTRE A mirror relieves the gloom by bouncing back the light opposite. It also "enlarges" the garden, filled with the tried and true shade-lovers for mild climates: philadendrons, ferns, aspidistra, spider plant, baby's tears and aluminium plant.

BELOW LEFT Shrubby hydrangeas create a sea of blooms in the shade throughout summer and will melt into autumn colour. Under-plant with naked ladies, maidenhair fern, cliveas or mondo grass, as here, to relieve bareness in the winter.

BELOW RIGHT In damp shade, baby's tears scramble with madonna lilies and sacred bamboo in pots. Star jasmine and sasanqua drape the fence, while a bird house and lantern complete the Oriental theme.

tiny garden
plant guide

Throughout this book, we've tried to
name each plant pictured and to use,
where possible, their common names
for easier reading and recall. Where
there's no common name, we've given
the botanical one. For example, on the
left is a large staghorn fern on a trunk,
a smaller elkhorn behind it, with a
many-fingered umbrella tree and a
marbled *Cordyline* 'Imperialis' cultivar
in front. This guide suggests just a few
reliable easy-to-manage plants that
will provide interest.

annuals

Annuals complete their lives in a year. Seed germinates, grows, flowers, new seed develops, then, job done, the plant withers and dies. They put on a great show of flowers to attract pollinators. How do you extend that show? Grow healthy plants in the right situation at the right time of year, always keep them watered and well-fed, pick the flowers whenever you can for the house, or a gift (this will stimulate further blooms), and trim off the dead heads to stop seed developing.

Tropaeolum majus

Bellis perennis
English daisy

A small deep green clump with single heads of white, pink or red daisies, flowering in spring and into summer. It remains neat and compact, flowers in light shade and may last more than one season.

Eschscholzia californica
Californian poppy

Bright yellow, orange, russet and red or creamy mixes now available give choice to tone with the design. Flat open flowers and grey feathery foliage, plus chance of reseeding for next spring/summer.

Cleome hassleriana
Spider flower

Usually pink-toned but pure white is also available. Plants develop a tall strong stem, 1 metre high, and the flower creeps up as it extends during summer in the sun.

Lavatera trimestris
Tree mallow

Not quite a tree, but shrub-like, they grow fast in full sun through spring in mild climates and are decked with mauve, pink or white open-trumpet flowers for summer. Reaches up to 50 centimetres tall and wide, but is upright and controllable. Perennial varieties are available, but using annuals allows you to move the effect about.

Primula malacoides

Cosmos bipinnatus
Cosmos

Warm weather flowers with flat, soft petals in red, pink and white tones with fine feathery foliage. Grows upright to 1 metre in full sun and good soil. Reseeds itself generously.

Portulaca grandiflora

Lavertera trimestris

Petunia x hybrida

Cosmos bipinnatus
(pink flowers)
Cleome hassleriana
(white flowers)

Nicotiana varieties

A relative of the tobacco plant, they're compact, perfumed and flower in summer in white, pink, mauve and lime tones – clusters of blooms with long trumpets.

Petunia

There are perennial types but these summer annuals have big flowers and masses of them when grown in the sun. Cut the flowers to prevent plants getting leggy. Colours range from purple, blues, pinks, reds, white and yellow with a variety of mixes available.

Portulaca grandiflora
Sun plant

Succulent stems and foliage will spread out neatly in spring, and by summer, gleaming jewels of flowers open daily in the sun. Great for pots and garden fronts.

Primula malacoides
Primula

Winter or spring flowering in most zones, with attractive rounded foliage that becomes obscured by long-lasting spires of flowers. Colours range from pinks and mauves to white in both sun and light shade. Polyanthus, another family member, produces bright heads of colour for shady corners.

Tropaeolum majus
Nasturtium

Some seeds can be purchased in specified colours, usually in the bright range. Some are compact and are probably best for small sites, others will climb and twine or drape. All have round foliage, while 'Alaska' has variegated leaves. For summer, they need partial shade or full sun. They will succumb to frost but there will be seedlings everywhere next spring. Take care not to overfeed them.

Viola varieties
Violas and pansies

These offer a low-growing and orderly winter to spring show in purples, mauves, blues, russet, almost black, pinks, yellow and white. Paint your scene with them in full sun to partial shade. Great for pots.

Lobelia erinus
Lobelia

Low trailing lobelia, with its purplish leaves and stems starts to flower in blue/pink/mauve or white in late winter and will continue into next autumn. Excellent for edging, pots and hanging baskets, in sun or partial shade.

perennials

Most perennials will last in the garden for a number of years. They'll need trimming back at the end of each season, dividing when they become too massed, generous feeding in spring and autumn to keep them robust, mulching to protect dormant roots or leafy bases from sun or frost, but, once planted, they'll present you with leafy growth and abundant flowers every year. What more can you ask of a plant?

Sedum spectabile 'Autumn Joy'

Agapanthus varieties

Clumps of dark green leaves will grow in most climates but will need protection against heavy frosts. They produce 1 metre stems during spring topped by a ball of massed flowers. Blue, white and pink tones available as well as compact forms.

Alchemilla mollis
Lady's mantle

Rounded leaves with crinkled edges are evergreen in semi-shade or sun in most climates except humid tropicals. Summer sprays of lime-yellow small flowers top the leaves.

Anemone x hybrida
Windflower

Evergreen divided leaves at base produce stems to 50 centimetres topped with buds in late summer. White, cerise or pink flowers open in autumn, swaying in the wind. Best in rich damp soil and semi-shade to sun.

Anigozanthos varieties
Kangaroo paw

From a dense clump of dark, strappy, evergreen leaves in sunny well-drained sites where water is regular, flower stems emerge in spring to stand about 1 metre above foliage. Coloured green, yellow, red and russet or pinkish tones, flowers endure most of summer. Dwarf forms are also available.

Helleborus varieties
Hellebore, Lenten/winter rose

Nothing like a rose, but a great winter bloomer for shaded, cool to cold conditions and rich damp soil. Leaves attractive and, like the flowers which stand above them and endure through winter, vary with species. Needs to settle in before flowering.

Pelargonium varieties
Geranium

Some shrubby, some trailing and some with distinctive leaf

Sempervivum cultivars

Rudbeckia fulgida 'Goldsturm'

Pelargonium varieties

Anemone x hybrida

Phormium tenax

markings, in mild climates they may flower all year. Just prune back to shape when needed. Most varieties prefer full sun.

Phormium tenax
New Zealand flax

Fabulous accent plant with a clump of upright straps of leaves. Colours grey-green, variegated and bronze toned. Some forms have leaves 2 metres tall, others are mere babies at 50 centimetres.

Romneya coulteri
Californian tree poppy

Divided grey leaves that may decline in frosty weather but will regrow once spring warms, the stems can reach 2 metres and are topped by white flowers with prominent stamens. Demands full sun but where it's humid, use cosmos or dahlias instead for flat white blooms.

Rudbeckia fulgida 'Goldsturm'
Coneflower

Bold, gold daisy shapes with conical black centres cover this plant in late summer/autumn. Cut back low when petals have fallen. In full sun with regular water it grows to about 50 centimetres in most climates.

Sedum spectabile 'Autumn Joy'

This succulent develops massed

stems that grow to about 30 centimetres each spring after dying back in winter. Leaves are fleshy and apple green. During summer a flat bud-top develops and opens in autumn with cerise flowers. Many cultivars available. Grows in sun or light shade.

Sempervivum cultivars
Houseleek

Select from the enormous range of colours and forms of this undemanding succulent. Grow in well-drained soil in full sun for best colour, in most climates.

Verbascum olympicum
Mullein

From a base of densely furred grey leaves, a 1-2 metre stem of yellow flowers emerges progressively opening upwards. Lasts a couple of years in full sun and will seed itself. Many other colour forms and heights are available.

Zantedeschia aethiopica 'Crowborough'
Arum lily

For semi-shade or sun where there is ample water, arums have year-round broad foliage and tall white lilies in spring and occasionally autumn. There is also a dramatic green streaked form, 'Green Goddess'. Wonderful as cut flowers.

groundcovers

These treasures clothe the soil and rocks with their leaves and stems while preventing wasteful moisture loss. They reduce weed-seed germination as the seeds can't reach the soil and will also hide any weeds that do grow. Most flower or have attractive foliage. Some mound, others creep but most don't grow above 30 centimetres. If they are invaders, control only means a quick trim or a dig around the planned perimeter in a small garden.

Viola hederacea

Ajuga reptans
Ajuga

Neat open cabbages of leaves in a variety of purple-green tones or mixes . Short spikes of blue flowers appear in spring. Needs dappled sun , well-nourished soil and plenty of water. It's easy to control.

Artemisia schmidtiana 'Nana'
Creeping wormwood

With fine grey foliage on stems reaching 10 centimetres, and small round yellow flower heads in late spring, this shrub likes sun and only light frosts. Acaena varieties with grey foliage will tolerate colder climes.

Erigeron karvinskianus
Seaside daisy

Small daisies open white and age to deep pink on a sprawling plant with tiny leaves in full sun in most climates. Clip regularly if neatness is required. It will reseed generously.

Gazania cultivars
Gazania

Select a variety to suit your summer scene, from the grey almost white leafed forms or grey-green, with bright flower colours ranging from orange and yellow to pink or white. Grow as an annual where the conditions are very cold or very wet; year-round elsewhere in full sun.

Grevillea x gaudichaudi

One of the many groundcovering grevilleas, this mounds to 30 centimetres and has red-tipped new growth. It copes with heavy frosts, dry conditions, sun and light shade but must be well drained.

Juniperus conferta
Shore juniper

A conifer to suit all climates, it forms grey tumbling mounds or drapes. Other junipers offer gold or bronze foliage.

Lysimachia nummularia 'Aurea'

Ajuga reptans 'Multicolor'

Erigeron karvinskianus

Soleirolia solerolii

Juniperus conferta

Lysimachia nummularia 'Aurea'
Creeping Jenny

In full sun the paired round leaves are yellow, becoming greener the heavier the shade. It does need regular water to keep it lush and will produce yellow flowers in summer.

Parochetus communis
Shamrock pea

For real shade and a cover 3-4 centimetres high, plant this clover-leafed blue-flowering wanderer. It needs water and can survive very cold winters when moved under cover.

Sedum acre
Stonecrop

This succulent produces a dense mat, 2 centimetres high, of tiny pale fleshy leaves. In spring and early summer it turns yellow with flowers. It needs full sun, can recover from frosts and doesn't mind dry conditions. It's easy to control.

Stachys byzantina
Lamb's ears

Grey woolly leaves form on 10-15 centimetre spreading stems, with blue-mauve 30 centimetre flower heads in summer. Prefers full sun and deep moist soil but tolerates dry conditions. Renew annually by planting some of the offsets or seedlings.

Soleirolia soleirolii
Baby's tears

A tiny cover for shade and well watered sites. Despite its delicate looks, it can spread aggressively but is easily controlled. It is shown here with ivy groundcover among stepping stones.

Thymus species
Thyme

Different varieties give alternatives for scent, height, leaf or flower colour and hardiness. All require full sun. Other herbs like golden oregano, chives and winter savory form neat and useful groundcovers.

Viola hederacea
Australian native violet

Widely recommended for shade but more flowery in sunlight, it grows in most climates and soils. It can be invasive but is easy to remove. New cultivars offer white flowers. Other violets are useful covers in shady areas but are more invasive.

Zephyranthes candida
Autumn crocus, rain lily

This bulb is evergreen and chive-like in all but the coldest conditions. Best in full sun or very light shade. Crocus-like white flowers appear after rainy spells and in autumn.

climbers

In this small collection are some of the less rampant climbers that can wrap, screen, beautify and shade your garden and your walls. Most of those we've mentioned won't be too difficult to control in a small area, although some are mentioned with warnings. Please take note of the advice. Varying conditions of climate, soil and position will result in performance differences, but remember that vines, by their very nature, need to wander about. They just can't help themselves.

Phaseolus caracalla

Ampelopsis glandulosa 'Elegans'

Variegated grape-like foliage unfurls in spring, insignificant flowers in summer, but in autumn the fruits ripen from green to dark blue to turquoise. Let it tumble on itself or climb a lattice. It lights up semi-shade.

Bougainvillea cultivars

Woody, thorned and scrambling climber with no real place in a tiny garden, the dramatic colours and flowering heads make a great impact against a wall. Prune it, feed it and shape it regularly. Delightful dwarf forms are available.

Clematis varieties

The range is enormous and will provide flowers of assorted mauve/pink/blue and white hues from spring into summer, with decorative seed heads. Most are deciduous and will need some control to keep them tidy.

Lathyrus latifolius 'Roseus' Perennial pea

Covered in masses of delicately scented blooms through summer into autumn, it shrinks back during winter to re-sprout in spring. It likes cool conditions and low humidity. The annual perfumed sweet pea flowers from late winter to early summer. Remove them when they become tatty and re-plant next autumn.

Hardenbergia violacea

Usually purple/violet clustered flowers through winter on this twiner, though pinkish and white forms exist. Will gently drape an arch or fence in mild climates.

Mandevilla varieties

A summer flowering vine that remains neat and compact and will grow happily in tropical, subtropical and Mediterranean zones all year but will need protection or replacement in

Ampelopsis glandulosa 'Elegans'

Lathyrus latifolius 'Roseus'

Bougainvillea cultivars

Pandorea jasminoides

Passiflora edulis

frost zones. Trumpet flowers in white, pink or reddish tones emerge from all stem ends.

Muehlenbeckia axillaris
Maidenhair vine

This wiry groundcover will twine itself upwards on any support. The circular, evergreen leaves are 1 centimetre across; stems are dark brown. It is easily controlled but keep an eye on it.

Pandorea jasminoides 'Lady Di'

This cultivar has white flowers in the warm months and is a bit more restrained in its growth than other pandoreas. Its evergreen, glossy foliage is attractive and long tendril stems point to where it's planning to go. You'll need to trim or direct them occasionally. Not suitable for frost zones.

Passiflora edulis
Passionfruit

An attractive evergreen and flowering vine that will need strict training and a radical pruning after fruiting to keep it tidy. It needs a tropical or subtropical climate.

Phaseolus caracalla
Snail flower

Fragrant, delightfully toned, snail-like flowers in cream and

purple appear right through the warm weather on this bean-like twiner, which must have warm conditions. You will also need to provide a steady frame for it to clamber up.

Wisteria varieties

Do not plant this in a small space if you are not going to be very strict with it. It can be trained upwards or feature as a standard and have its stems clipped as it wanders outwards. Flowers, foliage and form are varied and all are exquisite.

Senecio macroglossis
Natal ivy

Neat with small ivy-shaped fleshy leaves massed on thin twining stems. Yellow daisy-like flowers make accents through winter mostly, but sporadically all year as well. Do not attempt to grow this one in frost areas unless it is well protected.

Vitis vinifera varieties
Grape

Whether you're growing for fruit, for leafy shade or autumn colour, check your local nursery for what performs best in your area. A sunny site is all you need in most climate zones, as well as a good pair of secateurs and a solid frame to support the vine's considerable weight.

shrubs

Shrubs are the bulky solids in a garden – the shapers and the spacers, the scene-setters and, occasionally, the scene-stealers. Select them carefully for any of these roles as they can very easily overpower the site. It doesn't make much sense to plant a much-loved shrub if you're going to need to trim it constantly to keep it in line. You'll soon fall out of love with something so uncontrollable. Here we've listed some that are generally most obliging.

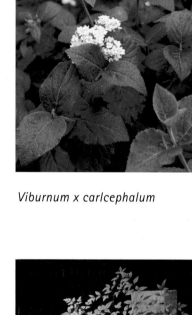

Viburnum x carlcephalum

Berberis thunbergii 'Atropurpurea Nana'

Its purple leaves are as dramatic as its autumn show and sculptural bare stems in winter. The form is small and won't need too much pruning – the spikes don't make it a pleasure. For most climates and full sun.

Cordyline fruticosa varieties

Many cultivars offer a choice of leaf colour, leaf shape and ultimate plant height. They do best in tropical and subtropical zones but can also provide a tropical look in protected sites in Mediterranean and even temperate gardens.

Cotinus 'Royal Purple' Smoke Bush

Best in full sun to develop rich leaf colour, they will flower in spring and develop smoke-like clusters by late summer. Autumn leaf colour is rich in cool climate zones. Don't feed it too generously or prune back hard if you want a compact plant, but provide ample summer moisture.

Fuchsia varieties

Numerous colour, leaf and form variations make these a possibility for any small garden. They prefer some shade, ample moisture and rich soil, and will flower right through the warm months. They die back in frosts but many will shoot again.

Nandina domestica

Gardenia augusta varieties

All richly leafed and bearing white flowers with heavy perfume in summer, they differ in size, flower form and growth habit. Select the variety that suits your needs. They need some sun, no frosts, generous feeding in autumn, and look best and flower more when yellowing blooms are removed.

Cordyline fruticosa varieties

Cotinus 'Royal Purple'

Hydrangea macrophylla

Lavandula dentata

Grevillea endlicherana

Fine grey leaves completely cover the numerous stems that can reach 2 metres tall and wide but will adjust to pruning. It needs full sun and good drainage and will flower with white/pink blooms along the nodding stems. Seed heads are round and purple.

Hydrangea macrophylla

These are the mop-head or lace-cap varieties that do so well in shade. They also need a deep root area and ample moisture but survive seaside, tropics and frosts. Spring to summer flowers gradually "rust" to autumn tones.

Ixora chinensis
'Prince of Orange'

For tropical gardens in part-shade, this low shrub will flower with orange/red clusters among deep green foliage for almost all of the year.

Lavandula dentata
French lavender

The short grey leaves and flowers are stouter than the English varieties. Leaves have an indented edge. In most climates there will be some flowers throughout the year, but winter is its peak. Lightly prune the bush regularly but avoid cutting into the woody stems. Replace when it gets unshapely for a compact specimen. Lavender must have full sun and any soil that is well drained.

Viburnum x carlcephalum

This rounded shrub to about 1.5 metres, is deciduous with autumn colour in cool zones, and white/pink blushed perfumed flowers in spring. There are many other forms to suit more climate zones but be sure that you select small growing varieties.

Nandina domestica
Sacred bamboo

Happy in most climates, semi-shade or full sun, this upright multi-stemmed shrub has soft compound leaves with long mid-ribs. It can reach 2 metres but has a delicate bamboo-like appearance. White summer flowers develop by autumn into red berries on the stem top.

Punicum granatum nana
Dwarf pomegranate

Slow-growing, compact, decorative and well suited to most climates, this shrub with its red flowers, autumn foliage and small, orange-red drooping globe fruits can be an unusual feature in the garden. It needs a sunny position, but does not demand much more.

small trees

Trees will be the anchor points in your garden. If they are growing outside your property and beyond your control, make them part of the design rather than excluding them. When selecting for your own garden, don't plant a forest giant. Choose something in scale with your area, that won't hem you in. Believe the information on plant labels in nurseries – it's expensive and disappointing to have to constantly trim or to remove a bad choice. Here are a few ideas to set you on your way.

Magnolia soulangeana

Camellia sasanqua

Although not officially trees, camellias with their trunks and crown of leaves atop appear tree-like. We've suggested sasanquas, as their small leaves, autumn flowers and delicate open form well suit a small garden. There are several other varieties of small-leafed camellia to substitute but for a space needing a dense, dark screen, japonicas and reticulatas are excellent too. They all adapt well to pruning.

Lagerstroemia indica
Crepe myrtle

When not pruned back to the trunk each year it will develop an attractively mottled trunk or trunks, with rounded leaves colouring in autumn, and masses of flowers in summer, a froth of white, mauve, purple or deep pink. In full sun it will grow to about 6 or 7 metres but can be shaped to reduce its bulk. It's happy in light frosts as well as in tropical zones.

Olea europaea

Eucalyptus caesia
Silver princess

This weeping eucalypt has a slender trunk with red/brown bark that peels off in curly strips. Branches, stems, fruit and buds are dusted white. In winter, its large red or pink flowers open. It needs full sun, well-drained soil and no humidity. Plantings of two or three look especially good.

Laurus nobilis
Bay

This is naturally a big tree but with topiary shaping, it can become an evergreen formal statement, either as a standard, a spiral twisting to a central peak, cut square, or as a group of several in a pleached hedge. Trim two or three times a year. Dry the leaves for the kitchen. Grow in full sun to part shade, in most climates and soils.

Eucalypyus caesia

Plumeria

Robinia pseudoacacia 'Frisia'

Malus x purpurea

Magnolia x soulangeana

These cupped blooms commence on bare boughs in winter in subtropical climates, but in spring elsewhere. More floriferous in sun, it will still bloom in light shade. It prefers deep rich soil with regular water. If your soil is sandy, add plenty of manure. Other colour and flower forms are available.

Malus x purpurea
Crab apple

With a crown of dense spring blossoms, summer shade, autumn leaf colour, reddish or yellow fruit and a strong winter leafless framework make this and most other crab apples useful trees for a subtropical to cool continental small garden. Height and spread vary so select a variety to suit your needs.

Olea europaea
Olive

Grey/green narrow leaves with silver undersides makes this tree arresting in the wind. It will grow slowly as it develops a clear trunk that can become gnarled and shapely with age. It will cope with conditions from the seaside to the mountains with some snow, in most soils. It also grows well in pots. Pale summer flowers develop into autumn fruit that can be brined for the table.

Plumeria acutifolia
Frangipani

For the tropics, subtropics and Mediterranean climates, these provide summer-long perfumed blossoms that scatter the ground, dense leafy shade and rugged stick-like framework where winters cause leaf-drop. Rosy pink and all-yellow forms are available, but all the flowers have a yellow throat.

Prunus serrulata
Japanese cherry

Smallish, compact and a great show stopper with masses of spring bloom and good autumn leaf colour. Provide rich, deep soil and ample moisture for robust and vigorous plants. Serrula, the Tibetan cherry, has a spectacular smooth red trunk that looks as though it has been carefully varnished.

Robinia pseudoacacia 'Frisia'

Golden compound leaves, at their richest in new growth in spring and autumn, before they're dropped from the draping limbs. It is fast-growing and rather too generously proportioned for a small garden but if you can fit one in, it makes a great impact, with its fragrant flowers and colourful foliage. Wayward boughs can be pruned off to keep growth more compact.

index